Rescuer Mindset

Michael Aloia
Brian P. Pasquale
Pamela Aloia

March Baby Publishing
First Edition 2011

Rescuer Mindset
Copyright©2011 by Michael Aloia, Brian P Pasquale, Pamela Aloia
March Baby Publishing
Collegeville, PA

All rights reserved. No part of this book may be reproduced, stored in a retrieval system or transmitted in any form or by any means, electronic, or mechanical, including photocopying, reading, recording, Web distribution, without the prior written permission of the publisher and author.

Disclaimer
The material presented within this book is based on the authors' observations and personal experiences. It is designed as a means to convey a personal opinion. Neither the publisher nor the author makes any claims, representations, warranty or guarantee to the success and or the effectiveness of the content described and/or illustrated in this book.

Additional copies are available online at *www.rescuermindset.org*
Library of Congress Control Number: 2011901470
ISBN: 978-0-578-07813-7

Editor: Macrina Russo
Illustrations: Michael Aloia
Layout & Design: A Creations Productions *www.acreations.com*

For more information:
Rescuer Mindset
Po Box 26452
Collegeville, PA 19426
www.rescuermindset.org
www.rescuermindset.com
www.asahidojo.com
www.solangel.com

Printed in the USA

Contents

Preface i
Introduction 1
SECTION I - THE CHOICE TO SERVE 3
These things we do 5
Compassionate Vigilance 9
Leadership Role 13
   Leadership, learning to support others 13
   Introduction to Leadership 14
   Awareness to Leadership 18
   The Power of Leadership 21
   The Role as Leaders 24
   The Leader is in You – Transformational Leadership 27
   Qualities of a Leader – Transcending Time and Cultures 30
SECTION II - STRESS THEORY AND PHYSIOLOGY 33
The Mind-Body Connection 35
   Alarm Phase 36
   Resistance Phase 39
   Exhaustion 40
Pre-Incident Stress Syndromes 43
   Cumulative Stress (Organizational) 43
   Attrition 46
Post Traumatic Stress Syndromes 49
   Extended Consequences 50
   Family Consequences 51
SECTION III – RESCUER DEVELOPMENT AND CONDITIONING 57
Maturity and Stress 59
Coping Mechanisms 65
   Humor 65
   Dietary Mechanisms 68
SECTION IV – MINDSET CONDITIONING 71
Principles of Self Protection 73
   Sensory Perception Training (S.P.T.) 79
Principles of Self Defense 81
   Verbal Defense – De-escalation 85

Rescuer Mindset

    Body Language 87
    Physical Defense 88
    Current State of Affairs 92
Aptitude for Training 95
    What is Quality Training? 97
Awareness Training 99
    Sensory Enhancement Exercise (S.E.E.) 102
    Sight 103
    Sound 105
    Smell 106
    Taste 107
    Touch 108
    Our Choice 109
Conflict Awareness and Avoidance 111
    Visualization 115
    Self Awareness 117
Conflict Resolution 121
    Give Way 122
    Change Direction 122
    Diffuse 123
    Modify and Adapt 124
    Go With It 125
    Get Out of the Way 126
    Connect 129
    Consider space and position – yours and others 131
    Don't allow yourself to be or get boxed in 133
    Become aware 135
Application 139
    Move, Connect, Control 139
    Distinction, Retention, Response 140
SECTION V - PREVENTIVE MEASURES 145
Stress Reduction - Clean Up Your Own House First 147
    Community Building 148
    CISM/CISD and War Stories 150
Physical Well Being 155
    Diet 157
    Sleep 160
    Resilience Training 162
Spiritual & Emotional Fitness 167

Maintaining Spiritual and Emotional Weight....................167
Mindset for Meditation 175
Stress Management 185
    Managing Stressors..185
Intuition 191
    Feel Your Way Around..191
Conclusion..199
Bibliography
About the Authors

Author legend
Michael Aloia:

Brian P. Pasquale:

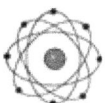

Pamela Aloia:

Rescuer Mindset

Preface

Mindset is a mental outlook or character that is preprogrammed and decides an individual's response to a variety of situations. It is the thing that, when all else fails - training, faith, intellect - makes something out of what seems like nothing or not possible. Mindset is a belief. That belief is success. Believing is success. Success is the ability to continue on come what may.

To define mindset is the easy part. To achieve a mindset befitting success is what becomes difficult. To change a mind is about the hardest thing to accomplish in our existence. To change our own mind, even when we may know of a better way, can be nearly impossible - our own patterned thinking can hold us back from making a needed mental change. There are those who exude an unstoppable mindset while others possess a waxing and waning mindset. Are we born with it – an innate coding written in such a way that failure of any kind is simply not an option? Is it a gene inherited and passed down from generations? It is possible that certain traits may enhance a superior mindset and tend to be common in those who display

Rescuer Mindset

such. But the mindset itself is a learned response – hence the use of the word "response" in the definition.

Certain inherited traits, if recognized early on, can contribute to the development of a proper mindset. With reasoning and deduction, these certain traits, such as drive, competitiveness, resilience and determination, only reinforce the positive nature of a "can do" mindset. These particular traits are often found in those athletes, entrepreneurs, world leaders, entertainers and doctors who are at the top of their field, always at the top of their game. However, mindset can be a learned state. Anyone, regardless of age, sex, religion, economic status and/or abilities is capable of great things and of great thinking. We just need to believe.

Where does one begin? How does one achieve the needed patterns to achieve the desired results? Rescuer Mindset has been written as the initial first steps to achieving such a mental state. This book helps the individual become more aware of others and themselves, and offers techniques to begin developing a positive, unstoppable mindset. Though geared towards those who work as Public Safety professionals: EMS, Police, Firefighters, *Rescuer Mindset* can be easily applied to any walk of life, employment and/or situation. The concepts are universal and interchangeable. It will then be up to the individual to adopt these doctrines as part of their everyday life as a means to accomplish and attain what they so desire. Believe and you shall succeed.

Rescuer Mindset

Introduction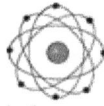

The nature of public safety work is inherently sedentary. With long periods of inactivity and boredom the EMS, police, emergency room providers or firefighters shift may be disrupted numerous times for calls ranging from the mundane the very traumatic. It is during this downtime that primary stress management mechanisms help rescuers maintain optimal states of readiness. Over the past twenty years more attention has been brought to the problem of traumatic stress issues related to emergency response work. As such, studies conducted have shown a multitude of stress sources involved in the public safety realm. High attrition rates within the EMS, fire, police and healthcare communities dictate that there is a need to develop an understanding of the prevalence of physical and psychological problems that plague public safety professionals.

Rescuer Mindset

SECTION I - THE CHOICE TO SERVE

> *Police*
>
> *…2:45pm, it's a quiet Sunday afternoon in November, a bit more frigid than usual this time of the year. Boy is it cold! As the holidays draw close, "down time" seems to be the norm. Today is one of those days. It's quiet, but may be too quiet - should be an easy day though. Well…couldn't be any more wrong. A call comes in about a disturbance on the lower east side… not where anyone wants to be on a day like today, let alone any other day. With no one else around… not much choice on who's going out…*

Rescuer Mindset

These things we do...

Consider for a moment the reason you, the reader, became what you are today. What was your reason? What compelled you to make that decision? Was it a need to be needed or more of a chance to give back to others? What difference did you believe your involvement would make? Has your presence made the difference you wanted or intended? How has your decision affected you as a person? Only you can answer these questions.

Those who choose the "rescuer way" answer a calling. It is a calling of service. That "calling" is one of service unto others. For others, your service is a chance at a better life. Yet the calling is not for everyone. Only a handful will answer and even less will make it a permanent vocation.

> *"That calling" - What compelled the more than 300 rescuers from NY fire and police to run into the doomed structures of the world trade center during the attacks of 9/11/2001, while hundreds of people were running past them, warning them of fire and destruction…it was "that calling".*

Rescuer Mindset

It may appear that this type of life holds more downs than ups, but at closer examination the difference you make, at times, could simply be a difference between life and death for the person you serve. The belief of making a difference is what fuels the Rescuer to do the deed each day without fail. Those base values continue to inspire and define the purpose and the need to be the one who serves.

Service, though looked at as a lowly, unfulfilling occupation by the general standards of today's material collective, is what truly demonstrates the real human character. Giving of yourself for another in need, who you may not know, is the human trait most often missing in the world of here and now and is anything but lowly and unfulfilling. Even as a needed addition to our society, our immediate community, it is not given the appreciation so well deserved. Yet there are those who make it their life's work. The need to make a difference, the willingness to lend a hand, the courage to stand up during times of need, these and many other qualities are what calls the rescuer to action. And it is by their actions, that others like them are inspired to join the cause and make a difference.

There will be times when the weight of what one does can become so heavy that the notion of giving up or moving on is considered. Whether it is the internal factors or the external ones, the decision to quit at one time or another confronts us all. How does one persevere? Are there self preservation techniques one can utilize so as not to become disconnected or just another statistic? Here are five suggestions:

- Believing is the first. Belief that knowing what you do does make a difference.
- Understanding is the second. Understand that as a rescuer, you are present at a moment in time most significant to the patient/victim/individual – possibly the lowest point of their day or life up until that point. This has great bearing on human reaction and interaction. Don't make judgments about others.
- Acceptance is the third. Accept that regardless of your intervention, you may not be able to "fix the problem", even given your best efforts and intentions, some things cannot be changed. Don't make judgments about yourself.
- Gratitude is the fourth. Be grateful for the opportunity to make a difference. Gratitude is rewarded not with open

Rescuer Mindset

    expressions of thanks and praise but in the subtle, quiet way that gives life a chance to go on. To serve others is recognition enough.

- Value is the fifth. Value what you do. Value others. Value who you are. Value is based on perceptions. And those perceptions can become skewed if we allow negative thoughts and feelings to overshadow our true beliefs. Believe that you add value to everything.

As uncanny as it may sound, service to others is service to one's self. To build a better world, some has to step up. The calling to serve the many outweighs the needs of the one. By that sacrifice, the world is made a better place. For those who put their time, effort and sometimes life on the line for the rest of humanity, the world is a much better place for all humankind.

Compassionate Vigilance

Everything we do involves the use of our minds. How we think of something has a great affect on what transpires in the real world. Positive begets positive just as negative begets negative. Opposites in this case really do not attract one another.

The mindset of any professional is the cornerstone of success and in some professions, the cornerstone to survival. What we think of others and often more importantly, what we think of ourselves is crucial in determining our actions when in regards to interaction. It is a process of being compassionate to the needs and wants of others while staying true to the needs and wants of ourselves. If we give of ourselves to others with no thought or concern for our own well being than we will often find it difficult to take the needs of others seriously.

Over time our demeanor becomes rote steps with no real concern, consideration or passion behind what we do. If looked at as helping others helps ourselves, then we are engaging in a mutually beneficial relationship, even if that relationship exists for a short time, it would bring meaning and fulfillment to our lives. Some may see these as being or becoming vulnerable and

Rescuer Mindset

allowing others to prey on our weaknesses. Compassion is not a weakness, but rather it is strength. In a world full of violence and distrust, compassion is an endangered emotional species, one that is slowly being eliminated in all walks of life. Lack of compassion begets more lack of compassion. Without it, humankind ceases to be human. And with that, professionals are no longer passionate about what they do. Without passion, things become routine and with routine there is no compassion.

On the same token, a mindset of vigilance is required from the individual. Vigilance, here meaning awareness, is essential for survival. It becomes a means by which professionals remain focused and safe. Vigilance offers an extended sensory perception. Vigilance is an accumulation of knowledge and experience, of time and sensitivity, of training and ability.

Vigilance protects the foundation of existence and ensures its survival. As professionals, vigilance creates the opportunity to engage effectively while maintaining awareness intelligently. But to be vigilant, individuals must be trained to do so. Vigilance is not an inherent commodity, it is a trained skill and one that can be learned, built upon and utilized by anyone. Vigilance opens not only the eyes, but the mind and heart, allowing the right decisions to be made, permitting the right actions to be carried out and providing the right care to be given.

As with anything, ample time and training is required to gather information, acquire the skill and acclimate that information and skill to a mindset. A mindset of *compassionate vigilance* offers both the necessary tools needed for self preservation and the ability to interact on a multifunctional level with one another.

Rescuer Mindset

Leadership Role

Leadership, learning to support others...

This text includes concepts of leadership as it pertains to and for you as a means to better enhance your professional management and interaction skills both physically and conversationally. Our goal is to offer a new perspective on how each of us builds and maintains relationships with others and with ourselves. As with any profession that deals with others; coworkers, management, as well as the public, certain criteria is required to effectively convey your thoughts, ideas and feelings to better serve the company, your team, the patient and yourself.

Defining what is real leadership as opposed to a role or position of command will set apart those individuals destined for greatness and those who are fated for the mundane. As with the previous chapters, recognition of the need and the resources to which to better one's ability, is knowing that it is essential for all of us – no one is exempt – regardless of position or post.

Betterment is available and it is obtainable. But, without the individual's intent to take advantage of what is available to them, nothing happens, there is no change, there is no betterment achieved. Leadership is set by example. Leadership is

Rescuer Mindset

the ability to inspire others. A leader is one whom others look upon to be inspired.

Introduction to Leadership

Adversity is part of human nature, part of human existence. Adversity exists. We must accept that. Great triumphs as well as great devastation have come about by adversity. Adversity with countries, governments, with people, environment and adversity with ourselves are all part of everyday circumstances.

Though existence is inherent of this adversity gene, we do, however, have choices of how we choose to deal with adversity. We may not see all our choices at the time but there are choices. Two common methodologies are to run away or meet it head on – the popular fight or flight response. Each, though widely accepted responses of fear and often given as excuses to explain human behavior, lead to nonproductive outcomes. Both tend to harbor emotional baggage and deep seeded resentment, be it externally or internally. When the current behavior options of fight or flight are rendered useless or lack the desired result, what are we left with? What choice do we have?

Before we reveal a third option, let's discuss that certain situations will require a fight or flight response. Let it be said that the fight or flight response has managed to keep our species alive for thousands of years. Circumstances will arise that require distinct actions and reactions as the results could be catastrophic otherwise. Of course we speak of life or death situations. As death is usually not a voluntary choice, the fight or flight response offers the choice at sustaining life. The choice we make to either run or engage needs to be one that we as the individual can live with after the dust has settled. Running from our fears or challenges can lead to emptiness and disappointment. Constantly colliding with what's before us can leave us drained and often angry.

To address the growing need for another course of action that will not only achieve peace externally but more importantly internally, we must consider the choice to harmonize. The decisions we make and the actions we take must sit well with us otherwise we are defeating the purpose and we face a life of regrets and frustrations – never to grow, never to live the life we want – the life we all deserve. To harmonize is simply that – find the commonality, find the similarities – find the harmony. Each of us is given opportunities each day to create peace – this is achieved on a one-to-one basis – a human level. That one-to-one

Rescuer Mindset

interaction carries over one person, one encounter at a time until it develops onto a worldwide level. But it all starts with you. We must view situations on multiple levels of perspective – others as well as our own. What are you bringing to the table that will enhance the situation or that will ultimately crush all efforts?

Sometimes unknowingly we bring a "multitude of baggage" and it can greatly affect and even be a detriment to what we set out to accomplish. Becoming aware of our perspectives allows us to be humble enough to accept the possibility of change. And if we can accept change, we can accept the view of others without judgment and without resentment. We truly view things as equal – we are one – we are harmonizing.

Before we can harmonize with others we must allow ourselves to harmonize with ourselves. Find balance within. Begin with letting go of what was and what has passed. Living in the past plagues all of us. "I could'ves", and "I should'ves" chain us down preventing us from moving forward. We become trapped in our own beliefs of negativity. The negativity leads us to believe we are not capable of more or better, leading us to not trusting in ourselves. And if we cannot trust ourselves, how can we ever trust one another? Let go, release yourself and accept that what has happened, perceived good or bad, has brought you to this point. And from this point on you will move forward. There is no yesterday, there is no tomorrow, there is only now.

> *Paradigms...*
>
> *It's 2 a.m. on a Saturday night and you receive a call for a "20 year old female" at a local bar complaining of "jaw pain." You sigh in frustration as you say to your partner "dude, Sandy is at it again!" You've picked up this local several times over the past few weeks. She states that she has general pain, tells you that ice and Tylenol don't work and the only thing that works is Fentanyl. Believing from your prior experience with her that she's only a "drug seeker", you arrive at the bar having rehearsed in your head what you'll say and spout out – "Sandy, get your ass on the bus and let's go!" Two weeks later you find out that she had surgery to correct a traumatic injury to her jaw that she sustained during an assault at the bar that night you picked her up...*

In order to get a clearer perspective we often need to create distance. Distance creates space and space creates time. Always rushing to the scene of the crime can cause a rote response regarding how we handle a situation. This opens the way to assumptions being made. Once we assume, we lose sight of what is really going on. We treat everything, regardless of the

Rescuer Mindset

situation, as the same. No distinction is made. In essence we become closed minded. Being open, in heart and mind, opens doorways to communication possibilities. And good communication is being well informed. Sometimes just knowing the facts can make all the difference and will greatly affect the outcome – ensuring positive results.

Awareness to Leadership

Knowing when distance is needed requires awareness. If you are too close physically to a person and it is making them uncomfortable, you need to be aware of this and change the distance. Walking around with our heads in the clouds results in confusion, misinterpretation and misinformation; missing our chance to harmonize. Awareness requires us to be connected to our environment. Not just seeing it with our eyes, but understanding it with our hearts and minds. Awareness allows us to connect with our environment on the levels we need to, at the times we need to.

Connect on a mental, physical, spiritual and emotional level to broaden the spectrum of understanding. Compassion, mercy, love, appreciation and gratitude are essential assets to develop, to expand awareness and connect us to our environments – home, work and social. This connection makes us aware of the subtleties – the inner most workings – of everyday living and interaction. Connection can be like a circle – it is continuous and unbroken – it is balanced. When we are connected, we are aware. Being aware leads to our ability to blend with what is taking place around us. It also allows that which is taking place around us to blend with us. Again, [awareness is] a continuous, unbroken circle – equidistant from its center – always flowing in perfect harmony.

Blending teaches us to consider the needs of others and in turn often fulfilling our own in the process. Blending allows us to find out the "whys". We all share similar feelings, thoughts, needs and fears. Quite often we are in need of someone just to listen. Listening can be a form of relating to the views of another. It is a form of respect. Respecting what they have to say and their need to say it. And, more likely than not, the ability to interact on a personal and positive level is achieved. Productivity is achieved. A mutual bond has been forged. Equality then is achieved. Equality is cooperation – everyone doing their part – no more, no less. We unite for and towards a common goal. We have blended.

Blending creates flexibility and adaptability. Situations can quickly take twists and turns in a blink of an eye. The means

Rescuer Mindset

to adapt and be flexible is key to continuous positive success. Be open, be honest, be fair, and be listening – to yourself and others. Don't act without thinking. Don't over react without being informed. If you find you have "gone blank" as a situation unfolds, take a step back, create distance, become aware and start the blending process again.

Clarity begets calmness as does the reverse. Confusion is then often followed by crisis. But crisis does not have to result in confusion. Adaptability and flexibility gives us the tools to be aware of our own need of change as well as the need to change a situation. They both serve to let us know when we need a break. No one is 100% all the time. Our awareness to our own needs will ensure ample rest and recuperation time is received, and with many of us, often neglected past the point of exhaustion. This will lead to poor judgment, oversensitivity and a lack of tolerance, thus hindering our discernment. Demonstrate flexibility, propagate adaptability with others and yourself and you will find it demonstrated with you in return.

The Power of Leadership

In any position there is a level of power – a level of responsibility. This power possesses energy and intent makes it either positive or negative. Those in power have the ability to alter lives positively or negatively simply by the decisions made, words used, and actions taken. Words and actions of a person in power can be a beacon or a blockade with regards to others. We either light the way for growth or we block the possibility of potentially propelling their life into new directions and to new heights.

Power is not negative nor is it positive. It is just energy and with all energy there is acceptance and responsibility. We accept what it is and take the responsibility for what it does and can do. How and what we choose determines the outcome. Parent, manager, coworker, student or caregiver; each possess a power of greatness – a power that can inspire and aspire. The power you have is nothing without the means to control and control demonstrates true leadership strength.

Strength is not merely the size of your muscles or the amount of weight one places on a barbell. Yes this is a measure of physical strength, and is only really relative to the person who is doing the measuring or being measured. Inner strength, however, is something that cannot be measured so easily. Each of

Rescuer Mindset

us posses extraordinary amounts of inner strength – whether we know it or not. Its range of motion is boundless. Depending on your lifestyle or simply your mindset, the depth of use of your inner strength will most certainly differ from person to person, and from moment to moment. Certain conditions will call upon different degrees of inner fortitude. That personal courage will be yet another determining factor in the outcome of a situation.

We all experience moments of internal fatigue – mentally, spiritually, emotionally – when the current state of affairs seems to be more than we bargained for. During these times of personal turmoil, the notion of giving up seems like the easy choice. With this one decision of quitting, everything will just cease – no more turmoil. Or so it seems. Making a decision to quit in times of trouble may seem like the answer at the moment – the popular flight response – but when the dust settles and the smoke has cleared, we are left with what has been done – our choice. And sometimes the choice we made is harder to live with than outcome of what would have happened if we stayed in the game a bit longer. When given the chance to shine and demonstrate our true potential, we took the easy way out. Our decision to quit eliminates our chance to see what we are really made of, to see if we have what it takes. Rather than fail, some decide to give up. Quitting leaves us with regrets and regret plagues us with questions that may never be answered.

There will be times when knowing when to stop something that is just not working will also require inner strength. Often, we can get so attached to something that we are blinded by it – so engrossed that we become consumed. And this could prevent us from seeing the true picture – that maybe things are not going quite as well as we hoped. Sometimes our passion and obsessive behavior can overshadow our ability to be honest to ourselves. Sometimes it can lead us to a dead end. Cases like these call for a change in direction not necessarily a change in destination. So the ability to determine when a change of course is needed is paramount for sustaining success just as staying true and firm to a chosen path that has some bumpy terrain is critical to succeeding.

In the shadow of our choices, true strength, however, is the ability to weather the storm and see the light through the impending darkness. Strength is always knowing that hope exists. Hope is the belief that things will be as we want them to be regardless of the present state of affairs. Hope, then, is the

Rescuer Mindset

strength of an individual's character. And character is one's innate way of always finding the silver lining. This will carry over as you interact with others. It will inspire others to aspire for something more than the mundane and in turn their actions will inspire to aspire others.

The Role as Leaders

In some contexts, where we position ourselves as a leader, in relationship to situations and with others, can have a dramatic impact on the outcome. At the center of the situation we can play two major roles: the first role being the pilot and the second being the target. In the pilot role we serve as ring leader or the one calling the shots. This role makes you the "go to guy" for solutions and solving. People look to you as an authority, as a leader. You involve others and offer the chance for their input. You are the leader of a team. Results and praise are shared. What you say and do has great bearing on the responsive nature of those who choose to follow – you have all the power. People want to follow. With this type of support, moving forward seems effortless if it is kept positive and constructive. You make the choice – you determine the outcome. But sometimes this role can easily flip flop into the second role, the role of the target.

Being the center may have its perks, but it also puts you at the center of the blame when things go awry. And in the eyes of others looking for someone to point a finger at, you become the source of the problem. Your interaction with others is less inviting. There is no team. You are an authority but one that does not invoke respect or equality amongst those who you lead. Your position exists to serve only you. Blame is handed down rather taken as a responsibility. This can rain havoc on your efforts for progress let alone dampen your own enthusiasm if you isolate others.

Putting yourself at the center has pros and cons and is only determined by your attitude. Are you a positive role model that makes others want to follow you? Or are you someone who forces others to follow using your authority as a sword? Your ability to listen and to be aware to what is really happening and what is really needed for the greater good of all will allow for positive results. Is it self-serving or selfless service?

The choice to listen especially in times of crisis is the silver lining. Often in haste we neglect to listen. A moment to listen may provide the answers. Don't just hear – listen. Hearing is passive. To listen is active, we actively engage in the

Rescuer Mindset

interaction. The choice to listen is solely your own. Good leaders listen to what others are saying. Great leaders build on what is learned through listening. When you take the time to listen to others you will find others more inclined to listen to you.

No one gets to where they are completely on their own. To some degree, others are always involved. No one really works walks alone. We share the road with many. How you involve them is based on the bonds of trust you make along the way – not just trusting others but trusting in yourself as well. Trust that you will make the right decisions, trust that you will be honest, open and fair. Trust that you will be trustworthy and respectful. When others are involved, respect is a mutual thing. You get as you give. Without it nothing gets done.

Respect places the needs of the moment, the needs of the crisis to the forefront rather than the needs of the individual or the needs of the ego. Involving others increases the chances of success. Mutually everyone sees the bigger picture. Respect is reciprocal and is the responsibility of all – leader and those being lead. Taking responsibility for our words and actions builds that mutual trust. It builds a circle of trust and within that circle answers are waiting to be found, spirits can be raised and progress can be made.

The Leader is in You – Transformational Leadership

The foundation of leadership is derived from knowing when to act and knowing when not to – both equally vital, both mutually essential to the others' success. Providing others a forum to express and relay their input only adds to your ability to properly lead. Correct timing will play a major role in your ability to act when change or decision is needed. If you get caught up in repeating the same manner of problem solving or relating to others as you have done in the past, you run the risk of repeating past mistakes. Each situation, though seemingly similar, are solely unique. Mistakes, on the other hand, are designed as a check point. They teach us new ways of thinking and doing. Mistakes expose us to new perspectives and reveal new directions. A leader learns from their mistakes.

A leader also always looks to fresh methods – fresh can be simply tweaking something old. A leader must be able to change direction at a moment's notice when the ability to progress has been halted. Changing direction energizes the moment. Without change the growth cycle ceases and so does the creativity and

Rescuer Mindset

focus. New methods do not mean changing the goal or the destination or disregarding it for another. Rather it is a means to find the harmony by letting go of the resistance. Finding the harmony is our way of finding betterment. Finding betterment ensures we are always growing. And as we find the betterment in ourselves, we will likely find the betterment in others. By the same token a leader must be committed to his direction – stable and balanced with every step – aware and in complete control.

The circle of trust completes itself. It is a give and receive paradox. To have it all we must give it all. To be all there is we must help others be all they can be. Our role as a leader is a life of service. Serving others serves us. We work towards the greater good. We allow others to be who they are by being ourselves – without judgment and without assumptions. To do this we must first accept ourselves and our role. We must own who we are and what we have chosen to do. We must own our position – we must own our personal power and use it for the empowerment of others – remaining centered, grounded and integrity intact. And for this to occur, we must take responsibility. We must hold ourselves accountable – morally, ethically, and spiritually.

To be accountable we must be worthy. Worth simply is a state of belief – it is an inward and outward projection of confidence and determination. Worth is a value you put upon something or someone – like yourself. Without it, it simply is just not worth doing. What are you worth? What is the real value? If you are unable to answer that, how can someone else? And if there is no worth, why would they bother to follow?

Real leadership begins in you. Not in a board room, or on a battle field or even in a family unit. Leadership itself is self motivated. It's knowing you can and you will – and that it is worth doing because you are worth it. This confidence is contagious and it is infectious. Real leaders are true collaborators. They are goal setters. They are cheerleaders. They are unstoppable. The goal to continually move forward keeps them alive and full of life and at the same time it keeps others kicking and living. Their goals keep them in the game never to be sidelined, never to be swayed. It keeps them winners.

The *Leadership Role* chapter is based on the book *How Aikido Can Change the World* and has been adapted for the purpose, content and subject matter of this book.

Rescuer Mindset

Qualities of a Leader – Transcending Time and Cultures
The following are modern interpretations of the Seven Virtues of Bushido – the Warrior Code of the Samurai as they appear in the book *Converging of Energies – Aikido's Path of Least Resistance*. True leaders demonstrate balance of the following virtues.

- With *integrity*, we come to learn the meaning of commitment. We exude a sense of justice in all things we encounter. We learn to be thorough and astute. We take pride in all that we do, all that we are.
- With *respect* we come to adore all life, completely appreciating the subtleties that surround us. We uphold the preservation of quality over quantity. Everything has value.
- With *courage* we face each day with wonder and eagerness. We do not settle for the mundane but turn each opportunity into a chance to grow. We never give up.
- With *honor* we allow ourselves to just be who we are. We are free of judgment from others and from ourselves.
- With *compassion* we are invited to be there for others when needed. We seek to make a difference in the world around us – one moment at a time.

- With *honesty and sincerity* trust is built. Trust yourself and others will trust you. Both your words and actions will move mountains.
- With *duty and loyalty* we become responsible. Our actions and our words hold great power and can be easily used to destroy. We take the responsibility not to misuse this power and stand to be counted in the wake of them.

Compassion – Japanese Kanji -
'caring for, understanding, desire to help, or listen to someone in need even if you do not know them'
A love for others and existence.
Compassion can also refer to charity

Rescuer Mindset

SECTION II - STRESS THEORY AND PHYSIOLOGY

> *EMS*
>
> *...1:22 a.m., finally with a chance to catch up on some much needed rest after being on continuous calls since 6 a.m. the day before, the station alarm goes off... again. It pierces through the early not so enchanted hour like a dagger. It always seems much more deafening when it's dark. In the blink of an eye and in an unconsciously animated state...the ride to the scene begins – as if teleported from the cot to the cab of the ambulance. The mind and body teeter between exhaustion and exhilaration – at times it is hard to distinguish the difference or if there really is a difference...*

Rescuer Mindset

The Mind-Body Connection

To appreciate the effects of stress, we must first consider the history and basic physiology of stress. We should consider that stress is a cumulative process; call it a cumulative injury or illness. Just as repeated and continuous exposure to asbestos, second hand smoke or other environmental toxins can lead to chronic health effects, stress although not necessarily measurable, can lead to a constellation of physical, emotional and psychological consequences which in severe cases can lead to death. This mind-body link has been acknowledged throughout history. Rene Descartes, in the 1600s, established some of the earliest ideas regarding the mind-body connection and human performance.

In the early 1900s, Hans Selye developed his theory of the General Adaptation Syndrome (GAS). In this theory he posited there are three primary stages of physiological response to stress, once again establishing the mind-body connection. The responses discussed under his theory address the mind-body relationship presented by Descartes nearly three hundred years earlier. Today leadership theorists and corporate leaders have focused their

Rescuer Mindset

interests on the relationship of the emotional, spiritual (mind components), and physical components of individual performance in order to improve longevity and productivity of their personnel.

Alarm Phase

Modern psychologists note the relationship of the mind-body responses to stress and continually try to analyze the most efficient ways for managing stress to prevent long-term adverse effects. The body utilizes the sympathetic nervous system to dump "stress chemicals" such as adrenaline into the body at a moment's notice during sudden stressful events. The physiological goal is to add strength to the muscles, increase breathing and cardiac efficiency, as well as to heighten the senses. The effects of the adrenaline dump cause the "unnecessary" bodily functions to be "de-emphasized" and depressed in many ways. Digestion slows, the skin becomes pale and the smooth muscles of the gastrointestinal system relax causing unique problems of their own. The modern study of this constellation of symptoms correlates directly to the "alarm" phase of the GAS theory.

Additionally, during chaotic or highly stressful situations, people will experience alterations in their senses. As some senses become enhanced during the event, other senses may be suppressed in the experience of the individual. Some prime examples include auditory exclusion or loss of hearing during events as well as experiences of "tunnel vision." EMS and emergency room healthcare providers often express experiences of "tunnel vision" during resuscitation efforts, particularly during orotracheal intubation. During the intense concentration period required to focus on the specific anatomical points involved, the provider sometimes loses perspective of time as well as the actions of others around them. The controversy of prehospital intubation involves the very discussion of time commitment to the skill application because it is something that is done during periods of high stress, adding risk to the overall procedure.

Rescuer Mindset

While on patrol during a military exercise with former Soviet troops, our team was engaged by a sniper. We were involved in this exercise for the purpose of training former Soviet troops peacekeeping operations for a near-future deployment to Bosnia and Kosovo. Although this was only an exercise, the intensity of the scenario had everyone on edge. The foreign soldiers readied their weapons and we got into a tactical formation and headed towards the suspected sniper's position. Above us hovered a Blackhawk helicopter, which seemed to be just above the treetops. As I made my way through the woodland scrub, I could hear the radio call sign from the helo above acknowledging "Lancer 4-3-7...over." All of a sudden, the tree line began to explode from all over...I could feel the rain on my helmet as I found the first point of cover, and brought my weapon to bear on the intended target. I could hear the counter-sniper team clearly on the helicopter radio calling in a fire support mission...my weapon was unusually quiet; typical it must have jammed! I looked down and performed my function check and everything was fine. I squeezed the trigger again. I was envious of the AK 47's used by the foreign soldiers as they made noise and my M-16 did not. When it all ended, I discovered that I had emptied my M-16, without any malfunctions and the "rain" I felt was the shower of shells from the door gunner in the helo above...yet I never heard a thing except the radio and those A-K's...

Resistance Phase

Studies of soldiers and public safety personnel continue to demonstrate standard responses to stress influences. Under the "resistance" component of the GAS theory, the ability for the individual to cope with the physiological effects of stress was known as "adaptive energy." The adaptive energy as described by Selye was correlated to physiological processes which could, if depleted result in "tissue damage." The discussion of adaptive energy is considerably close to the discussion of sympathetic release of adrenaline into the body. The extended release of adrenaline, under sustained stressful conditions is likely to cause hypertension, heart disease and in some cases acute coronary syndromes.

If we take a modern perspective regarding "adaptive energy" we can correlate this to wellness and stress training. Modern science has taught us the tenets of healthy living and how things such as good diet and exercise build upon one another in order to alleviate or reduce the cumulative effects of stress. In the professional lifetime of the average rescuer, whether in the hospital, on the street or on the battlefield, we will lose colleagues and friends to things that we can't believe killed them. How many times will we attend a funeral and say "[s]he

Rescuer Mindset

was so young...I can't believe it." It is during this phase that the ugly head of stress is beginning to rear itself and truly take its toll on your health.

Exhaustion

Sustainability of the resistance phase is individually based on the person's stress resilience. Increased stress conditioning, stress management training or "resilience training" will enable high performance occupations personnel such as public safety responders to maintain higher performance levels under stressful circumstances, with less adverse effects. The exhaustion phase was expressed by Selye as "the depletion of adaptive energy" and he presented the possibility of death as an end result. Studies of law enforcement and military personnel responses to incidents did illustrate evidence that corroborates the discussion of both exhaustion and the possibility of death. In high stress cases involving disaster response or law enforcement personnel who had executed "high risk" missions, several accounts have been presented of rescuers having "passed out" at the close of the mission due to exhaustion. Despite the relatively short duration of the mission, the stress factor resulted in increased sympathetic nervous system activity resulting in a natural "adrenaline rush" for performance followed by a post-incident "crash." This "oscillating" method of energy production and release is the premise for emotional homeostasis.

Inspired by the painting "The Ecstasy of Saint Francis of Assisi" by Sigismondo Coccapani c. 1600

Rescuer Mindset

Pre-Incident Stress Syndromes

Public safety and corporate leaders continually search for ways to make their systems more efficient within these times of diminishing budgets. As such, the strain of doing more with less takes its toll on their providers. This is not a phenomenon unfamiliar to any corporate entity. Leadership theorists continually seek ways to increase performance of employees while trying to identify who will flourish and who will fail under the cumulative effects of stress. It seems that there is a higher risk of stress sequelae during periods between critical incidents where an accumulation of stress occurs based on organizational and occupational factors with both subtle and insidious onsets.

Cumulative Stress (Organizational)

How many times have you heard someone say "[s]he snapped after the incident?" Many in the public believe that rescuers are victims to incident related stress as an occupational hazard and don't consider the concept of cumulative stress. Working in chronically stressful and dysfunctional environments can make rescuers more susceptible to the development of PTSD and is attributed highly to the high personnel turnover rates within the public safety professions. Sources of cumulative

Rescuer Mindset

organizational stress include low social and managerial support which, in turn could prevent expression of emotional problems. The physiological results of this "bottled up" negative stress could lead up to increased levels of anxiety and depression which exacerbates the physiological response leading to the release of those previously mentioned stress-chemicals. Contrary to popular belief, studies show that cumulative organizational stress was a larger factor in the development of PTSD and psychological anomalies in rescuers than incident-related stress.

Typical sources of organizational (cumulative) stress within the rescuer community include increasing call volumes, accompanied by poor organizational response mechanisms (increased workload), "nuisance" calls, changing schedules or shift work, changing coworkers (partners), as well as inadequate stocking or poor maintenance of equipment. These factors transcend the contexts of the hospital emergency room, EMS, fire, police and so on. Additionally, rescuers are frequently subjected to disproportional scrutiny for "quality assurance" purposes and ultimately an overall lack of respect is sometimes felt by rescuers on the part of the public. How many times have victims, patients or others expressed their dissatisfaction on what was not done for them - "My taxes pay your salary, therefore...." All of these factors continually exist within organizations and are inherent to the job regardless of context. It would seem that by pure nature of the healthcare and public safety industries, uncommon tours of duty, rotating partners, ever-changing equipment accompanied by compromises in pay, equipment integrity and logistical resources are all destined to remain factors in most agencies that will continue to significantly and adversely affect job satisfaction.

Job satisfaction surveys in the EMS and healthcare communities have historically indicated that organizational stress and overall job satisfaction remain the primary ingredients to provider attrition. The simple precepts of individual motivation as established by Abraham Maslow's theory of motivation need to be addressed in order to mitigate preventable loss. Personnel in these surveys indicated issues surrounding role ambiguity, self esteem, job security, sense of community, self worth and long-term planning were key issues of consideration. Many of these personnel surveyed identified that within the paramilitary structure of their departments (whether fire-dept. based EMS, EMS stand-alone or hospital ER), their primary complaint was lack of appreciation within their organization. It would seem that

Rescuer Mindset

regardless of union representation, many of these personnel did not feel as though they were integral parts of their respective organizations, with legitimate input regarding the successes of the organization. In retrospect, looking at the typical structure of police, fire and EMS units specifically, the paramilitary culture with which they are typically run does not routinely provide for a transformational leadership model, which may ultimately lead to personnel dissatisfaction, and ultimately attrition.

Attrition

It has been suggested that long-term cumulative effects of stress can lead to increased rates of absenteeism, chronic illness, increased healthcare utilization rates, disability and ultimately premature death in rescuers. Some estimates of attrition within EMS alone project a loss of nearly half of the rescuers within the first 2-5 years of their entry into the field. Ironically, there is little evidence that incident-related stress was causal in these attrition rates. It seemed that most accounts of rescuer loss were based on organizational cumulative stressors, many of which were preventable.

Previously discussed, the high dissatisfaction rates of healthcare, EMS and law enforcement personnel were typically oriented in a perception of the lack of appreciation for their contributions to their respective organizations. Although union representation may have offset other contributing stress factors such as pay, benefits, time off as well as managerial issues, union representation may also represent collective attempts to identify and mitigate organizational stressors. In short, leaders should consider unionization a proverbial "cry for help." The astute leaders will recognize the cry for help and should begin the assessment of cumulative factors and identify those which can be directly affected by organizational change. It is the prevalence of these cumulative stressors upon the rescuers that may make them prone to the development of post-traumatic or incident related stress syndromes and ultimately losses to the organization.

Rescuer Mindset

Post Traumatic Stress Syndromes

Post traumatic stress disorder (PTSD) is defined by the American Psychological Association as an anxiety disorder characterized by an individual who has experienced or perceived an event that threatened death, serious injury or other significant harm to self or others. Participants of focused studies indicated some of the events related to their perceptions of harm included violence against themselves, line of duty deaths, multi or mass casualty incidents, death of patients in their care and death of children. Too often the term "PTSD" is thrown at personnel in healthcare and public safety as a catch-all diagnosis to label behavior not commensurate with expected performance after a traumatic or dramatic event.

The reality of healthcare and public safety occupations is that these scenarios are not too uncommon, and that death of patients under pre-hospital care is not only a reality, but an inevitable probability. Repeated exposure to traumatic events has a sensitizing effect being cumulative in nature itself, and considering the previously discussed inevitability of exposure to such incidents, it is likely that rescuers at some time will experience stress-related syndromes. Now considering that

Rescuer Mindset

rescuers are subject to multiple genres of cumulative stress, it would seem difficult to pinpoint the specific causal factor in the development of adverse reactions over the course of time.

Consider this: Incident-related stress and repeated exposure to traumatic events result in a "sensitizing effect" according to psychology professionals. Yet, we see that in veteran rescuers well developed coping mechanisms seem to make them "invulnerable" to the effects of traumatic incidents. We should then suspect that as the "desensitizing" coping mechanisms become more prominent in the rescuer's personality and behavior that in fact, the cumulative effects of stress are "chipping away" at the proverbial "armor" that the veteran rescuer has developed.

Extended Consequences

Organizational consequences begin within the agency, as cynicism develops towards the rescuer for their repeated requests for time off due to physical or psychological injury. Leaders and managers begin to feel the effects of increased rates of personnel call outs, employee illness as well as decreased productivity, efficiency and performance. Other employee morale begins to suffer as they bear the burden of changing schedules, increased workloads, disruptive rumors as well as administration of punitive measures implemented as a result of some cases of delinquent behavior, not necessarily their own. As time progresses and organizational stress sources are not addressed or individual resiliency is not developed, legitimate physical injuries, chronic illnesses and in extreme cases even death can ensue. Additionally, with regards to organizational morale and support, negative attitudes and responses to anomalous behavior on the part of the stress victim are potentially infectious to others within the organization. Additionally, negative behaviors can be brought home and passed on to their family members.

Family Consequences

Mentioned earlier, rescuers and healthcare workers are subject to a multitude of job-related stress, yet in families where the members are not in the same or similar occupations stress symptomatology can be found in the family members of these rescuers. Statistics vary, but nearly half to two-thirds of paramedics claim being assaulted on the job, or they had responded to incidents that could have lead up to their own deaths. The accounts for in-hospital emergency providers in some estimates are event higher…and law enforcement, higher yet. The effects of stress, whether cumulative or incident-related as in the claims above are not solely left for the individual to deal

Rescuer Mindset

with, but rather they become contagious affecting those closest to the individual such as the immediate family members.

Later in this discussion personality traits and coping mechanisms such as emotional distancing will be discussed. What is important to consider about these popular coping mechanisms is that they are typically contradictory to the needs of the rescuer's family. Typically an emergency worker is a "type A" personality, which hallmark traits include immediate decisiveness, independence and skepticism. Those inherent traits and associated skills do not necessarily foster the communicative needs of spouses, children and the family structure ultimately predisposing rescuers to possibly higher rates of separation and divorce.

Desensitization, "emotional distancing" or "mind numbing" mechanisms often adopted by many veteran emergency workers focus on enhancing performance by allowing them to concentrate on cognitive aspects of the job rather than the emotional connection to the victims or families. These involuntary coping mechanisms again may diminish the rescuer's ability to connect with the emotional needs of their own children and family members. Consequently "lack of emotions" will likely prevent the emergency worker from experiencing good "family time." Considering the "cold" state that develops, it can be reasonably expected that there will be reciprocal negative feelings by the family towards the individual regarding their relationship and ultimately the emergency worker's occupation.

Cases exist that show researchers who review accounts of traumatic incidents can eventually experience signs and symptoms of traumatic stress related to their incident reviews. When an emergency worker returns home and consistently inundates their spouse with stories and accounts related to job stress, one can reasonably expect a degenerative effect on the family. Researchers who are trained and akin to the effects of cumulative stress demonstrated their own adverse responses to disinterested case reviews, therefore one must reasonably expect that families who are not trained in stress recognition and mitigation may demonstrate their own adverse responses to the constant battery of stressful stimuli. What makes matters worse is that the family is emotionally vested into the healing process of their loved one, therefore the natural coping mechanisms developed by many veteran emergency workers are not

Rescuer Mindset

necessarily available to families based on their sheer emotional attachment to the story teller.

One of the plagues of public safety work is the uncommon tour of duty and shift work. Many families are troubled by the propensity for emergency workers to be held late due to the unpredictability of calls near the end of their shift. Unpredictability sometimes forces the imaginative creation of concerns about rescuer safety or infidelity on the part of the "at home" family members. With the availability of television news twenty four hours per day, pictorial images of police shootings, building fires, disasters as well as general acts of violence do not lend any form of comfort to those waiting at home for loved ones. Again, another form of cumulative stress is impressed upon family members of rescuers based on the regular availability of television news coverage.

It seems particularly difficult to imagine a loved one spending more "awake" time with someone of another gender while at a workplace that in many cases has living amenities such as private bunkrooms, kitchens, co-ed bathrooms, etc. The public safety and healthcare communities have been wrought with sexual innuendo, banter and discussion, which may, in turn take a negative toll on relationships at home.

Rescuer Mindset

SECTION III – RESCUER DEVELOPMENT AND CONDITIONING

> *Fire*
>
> *…it's like there is something in the air. There's no warning signs - everyone just knows something's going to happen; not sure where or when, but it's going to happen. It's just a waiting game now. The recent rash of random calls appears to be turning into an epidemic. The trucks are continuously being called out…around the clock. These aren't just a small accidental kitchen calamity… these are blazes of grandiose proportions to those who are wondering why this happened to them. Just hoping no one gets seriously hurt…*

Rescuer Mindset

Maturity and Stress

"Newbies" may be their own "worst enemies" with regards to predisposition for cumulative stress. The newly qualified rescuer is typically enthusiastic about the job and spends every minute waiting on "the big one" to come along. In their excitement, many spend inordinate amounts of time in wait, fearing the possibility of missing the "good one." Fortunately for society, most systems are not that busy with highly traumatic incidents and the majority of emergency work remains centered in the mundane and ordinary. Unfortunately for the new emergency worker, the cumulative stress effects of these "nuisance" calls do take their toll over time, becoming a contributive factor towards burnout.

Stress can be a positive motivating energy, especially in newcomers compelling them to high levels of performance. Conversely, the lack of positive stress can lead to feelings (negative emotions) of depression, displeasure, sadness, low self-esteem and misery. Considering the possibility that the absence of positive stress can lead to adverse mental states, and the overabundance of negative stress can be detrimental as well, then

Rescuer Mindset

individuals must be able to recognize and determine the level of stress that positively impacts their overall performance and wellness. Keeping in mind the concepts of positive stress should help leaders understand that harnessing or enabling the newbie to exploit their positive stress (energy) is healthy for the worker and considered good for their overall wellness. Many believe that leaders who take use the positive motivations of the newbie in a synergistic fashion are taking advantage of them and leading them to an earlier burnout, whereas in fact, they are actually promoting and sustaining wellness behavior in the emergency worker.

The rescuer is often caught in the proverbial "tug of war" of occupational philosophies. When the individual initially decides to pursue a life in public service, it is typically based on several intrinsic factors wrapped in the guise of selfless service. They are called to perform acts not typical of human behavior, not out of fear of reprisal or penalty, but rather out of servitude towards the unit, group or community. We find that in military, police, fire and EMS there are often groups and subgroups within agencies known by names such as "the brotherhood." It is the herd mentality or "espirit de corps" that motivates these folks to do the unthinkable, and not the promise of reward or penalty.

The rescuer typically exhibits the "type A" personality which is characterized by passion for their cause, independence and self-motivation as we previously discussed. The dichotomy of public service, whether fire, police, EMS, or otherwise is that most of these organizations are characterized by a paramilitary structure which orients itself to strict chain of command and authority rather than individualism or independence. Even in the hospital emergency room environment, the corporate organizational structure leads to patterns of overregulation and "mother-may-I" processes that inhibit providers from "stretching their legs" per se. Those relationships of the newcomers to these organizational cultures are initial sources of adverse stress upon the emergency worker.

Burnout is a culmination of the stressors over time resulting in emotional exhaustion and chronic state of diminished interest. It is often identified by poor attitudes towards others as well as job essentials, poor work performance, and chronic health issues. Hallmark presentations of the burned out worker are exhibited by rude and disruptive behavior within the

Rescuer Mindset

organization. We see the projection of anger and frustration towards others in an effort to in some way alleviate the displeasure of their own miserable experience. The emergency worker is like a tea kettle with negative stress being represented as heat and water being energy. In the burnout phase, the tea kettle is boiling and the water, now charged with negative stress (heat) is spewing onto everything and everyone around it. Cooling represents positive stress or healing, which ultimately keeps the water inside the kettle.

Burnout can be correlated to Hans Selye's exhaustion phase of his GAS theory. If chronic health issues are not addressed, Selye's posit that death can occur during this phase can be validated. When an emergency worker is successfully able to avoid burnout by successfully adopting coping mechanisms, then resilience can be achieved for career longevity.

Resilient behavior is developed as a rescuer matures beyond burnout in their career. The resilience phase may be marked with a lack of enthusiasm (positive stress influence) for the job, yet it would differ from the burnout phase simply by allowing or accepting what was once considered a nuisance as being "the norm." In short, the emergency worker becomes more "flexible" in their perspectives and more "tolerant" in their behaviors. What is seen over the maturation of a long rescuer career typically begins with an abundance of positive stress influence, ending an abundance of cumulative or negative stress leading to burnout. If the rescuer does not depart from their career field, coping mechanisms, such as complacency and mere tolerance can likely develop, which may mitigate both positive and negative stress influences alike.

Caution must be exercised during the resilience phase. Acceptance of the "norm" or complacency can inhibit attention to details once brought on by enthusiasm and positive stress. In the realm of the emergency worker, even the smallest details can lead to tragic results. In the case of "Sandy" previously discussed, the crew failed to perform a detailed interview and assessment of the patient, dismissing her request as another attempt at getting pain medications. Although, this case did not have a tragic ending regarding loss of life or limb, it does reflect a moral or ethical issue with regards to providing patient care and comfort.

Rescuer Mindset

Coping Mechanisms

Dissociation mechanisms frequently developed by veteran rescuers often contribute to the development of PTSD. Emotional distancing is ingrained into the emergency worker cultural mentality (as well as the military) establishing that an individual must be mentally "tough" to be effective on the job. As such, many veterans unwittingly develop emotional distancing mechanisms which are a means of suppressing natural emotional responses to stressful situations. Unfortunately, evidence suggests that this coping mechanism only holds immediate value and the cumulative effects of this mechanism actually lead to the probability that the emergency worker will go on to develop later stress-related disorders.

Humor

Humor and cynicism have long-since been recognized as stress-reduction mechanisms that have been widely accepted by the emergency worker culture. It is not out of the realm of possibility to find responders giggling and laughing in the midst of a stressful or traumatic incident. Historically, stress has been linked to laughter, especially when considered in the context of anxiety, sympathy and fear. Laughter is thought to be an

Rescuer Mindset

unconscious result of a subconscious attempt to conceal fear or anxiety. The discussion of humor for our purposes relates to the specific coping mechanisms adopted by emergency workers. It serves as a sign of general stress coping, emotional exhaustion, as well as annoyance in the contexts of either organizational or incident-related stress.

It's Tuesday afternoon, on a hot summer day. The alarm sounds for a subject in pain. The ambulance rolls, lights and sirens to the call for a 50 year old woman with generalized pain. Pre-arrival instructions reveal a hospice patient who is experiencing increased general pain and wants to be seen at the hospital for comfort measures.

I respond in my officer vehicle to assist the crew. Upon my arrival I find a veteran female paramedic and EMT at the patient's bedside. The patient is writhing in obvious pain. She has pancreatic cancer which has spread and she's already on narcotic pain medications for her condition. The paramedic attached the cardiac monitor to find the patient's heart rate to be over 200. What started out as a comfort measure call has now elevated in criticality. The patient's blood pressure is not able to be obtained, and due to the poor physical condition, IV attempts were unsuccessful, her indwelling vascular port was inaccessible with our equipment and overall, there's nothing we could do. All of a sudden, the paramedic as she's trying to explain to the patient and her husband the severity of the situation, she began to laugh and chuckle at the end of her sentences. She was obviously unaware, yet she was genuinely concerned and visibly worried about the patient's condition.

In no way did she mean any disrespect...

I addressed the family in another room while the crew evacuated the patient and transported her to the hospital of choice for the family. I assured them that the paramedic is one of the best and more importantly the most conscientious and her laughter was one of worry and not entertainment...

Rescuer Mindset

It is unclear whether the personality traits of rescuers predispose them to the effects of cumulative or traumatic stress. It is to say the least that soldiers, police and emergency workers alike try to maintain "hardened exteriors" in the face of chaos or impending doom per se. As previously discussed there is a likelihood that these responders will not express their emotional distress or anguish to others fearing the cultural stigma of being "weak" or incapable. Humor or laughter regardless of the externally perceived appropriateness (or lack thereof) provides the needed unconscious cover for the individual to hide their stress while externally expressing it.

Dietary Mechanisms

Previously mentioned in this book, emergency work is frequently wrought with long periods of down time. When not properly managed, the stress of boredom can lead to poor dietary habits based on the perceived need to combat fatigue in order to maintain sensations of optimal readiness. One should consider the neurochemical dependence that processed sugar establishes during chronic consumption. First and foremost, the physiological response of the body and brain are to release the "feel good" biochemicals such as dopamine which give an immediate sensation of satisfaction to the individual. These are similar feelings of satiation felt by drug addicts who get their "fix" at the end of a needle or crack pipe. While the drug addict is "chasing the dragon," the emergency worker is chasing the energy boost for performance and stability on the job.

The metabolism of processed sugars leads to the massive release of insulin for sugar utilization, resulting in an immediate feeling of a "high" or heightened level of performance. The paradox of processed sugar consumption for performance is that the bolus of immediately available sugar supplies are quickly exhausted, while long-term complex sugars remain stored within the body, due to the exhaustion of insulin stores leaving the individual feeling depleted and craving another sugar or caffeine "fix." This proverbial "rollercoaster" has obvious short-term as well long term adverse effects on overall health and wellness. Since the chemical makeup of sugar is so close to that of ethanol alcohol (contained in adult beverages), the addiction potential for sugar is similar to that of alcohol.

Long-term use of processed sugar products by emergency care workers may lead to physiological consequences similar to those of alcohol dependence. Additionally diabetes and heart troubles can develop. Constellations of minor maladies can occur

Rescuer Mindset

including gastrointestinal disorders such as irritable bowel syndrome. Mood swings and personality changes are known to occur in the sugar-addict. Ironically, processed sugar addiction has been considered the leading addiction in the US, contributing to several public health epidemics such as pediatric obesity. With this knowledge, one must wonder why the educated emergency worker population is yet still so addicted to processed sugar.

Considering the evidence, the long-term demand for sugar usage will only increase over time in order to achieve desired energy responses, while the adverse effects of sugar consumption takes its toll on the body. Therefore, the rescuer must be educated to the actual effects and consequences of sugar as well as other "performance enhancing" agents, and balance their consumption to mitigate their associated adverse effects.

SECTION IV – MINDSET CONDITIONING

> *ER Nurse*
>
> *…It must be the full moon tonight…everyone and everything seems to be coming through that door. There hasn't been a time to just sit and breathe in hours. Who's been shot, who's been stabbed, who's having a quarrel with their spouse, who's tired of living… It's a broken record, same song different day. It's like no one even wants to try and get along anymore. Maybe it's something in the water. Maybe it is just time for a career change…*

Rescuer Mindset

Principles of Self Protection

In light of the chaotic nature of our present day world, the growing need for individuals to possess the tools to protect themselves in the event of a physical encounter is growing at increasingly alarming rates. Many of us tend to neglect this need, believing that "it cannot happen to me". But the reality is that it can happen and does to handfuls of innocent, unsuspecting citizens every day.

Self protection is not a means of being a war machine or becoming a god-like physical specimen. Rather, self protection can be simply changing your mindset, enhancing your focus, learning to adapt and modify, understanding the concepts of defense and familiarizing yourself with basic, fundamental movements that can ultimately save your life.

Self protection is a means to keep yourself out of harm's way when at all possible, preferably all the time – it is a mental state. It is a conscious decision to make a subconscious intent to a keep a respectable distance and avoid conflict regardless of how small it may seem. The smallest of conflicts can easily inflate to the largest of dilemmas with a variance of consequences – none of

Rescuer Mindset

which result in anything positive. The personal mindset to be vigilant about self protection is one only the individual can make and only one that the individual can be disciplined enough to maintain. It is not a temporary choice or a quick fix, self protection is a lifestyle decision. Its decision will affect every aspect of the individual's being and existence.

Day to day routine will not be just routine; it will be a way of life – a code of survival. It will become a calculated, but instinctive response for your daily course of action and interaction. Quality of life will be determined by your means of survival. This is not stating that the individual becomes that of a militant mentality, living in a life of seclusion and obscurity but rather living vigilant and aware. Situational Awareness Situational awareness is the backbone of self protection. Situational awareness, or scene safety and awareness, is the comprehensive attentiveness to the very fabric of what is going on around you and the omnipresent premonition of what can happen. It is a perception of the "here and now" as well as the "what is to come" or "what if". Situational awareness leads to better thinking and better decision making. Environments are a constant changing world, especially those in crisis, thus, the awareness to is constantly needed to be maintained and the information received reorganized. Like finding a needle in a haystack or a diamond in the rough, awareness is in the specifics. Awareness is a grouping of assessment, focus, understanding, reassessment and response – repeated over and over again as the situation unfolds and an end is reached or achieved. Attention to detail will serve to enhance the mental computation. See what is going on, mentally grasp it, properly respond as needed and offer appropriate solutions of resolution. Situational awareness affects not only you but others as well. The goal is safety and security, for the individual, the team, for the area – here, now and beyond. Further development of this topic is discussed in the *Awareness Training* and *Conflict Awareness and Avoidance* chapters. Understanding **what** we see - seeing and understanding are not necessarily the same thing. One may see or notice something out of sorts, out of character, but is not able to process a coherent mental picture as to what is really taking place. Misinterpretation can be disastrous. What you see, how you see it, how you interpret it, how you act on it, how you respond to it, the decisions you make and carry out affects everything.

Rescuer Mindset

Situational awareness then takes on a clear and firm understanding of what is really transpiring. The ability to read between the lines is the understanding skill needed to define the measures of response. Situational understanding is then the ability to respond in a clear and concise manner befitting what is taking place based on the information observed and obtained. Clear and concise can also refer to one's ability to see and understand the situation for what it is, not what they make it out to be.

Proper and accurate judgment is not impinged upon personal stereotypes, prejudices, likes, dislikes, opinions, fears or indolence – a true and honest evaluation, where the goal is success. Understanding is more than just experience, it is empathy. It is compassion. It is not being naïve regardless of your time in. It is vigilance. It is a mode of reasoning and deduction that poses the questions: how, why, when, where, and who not just what. Rather than asking "what happened", search for the deeper meanings as "how did this happen, why did this happen and who did it happen to?" These specifics hold the answers – all hidden in plain sight. It is the understanding of the things you are made or become aware of that explains the situation you encounter as you rush to save the day.

Pertaining to others and yourself, situational awareness is a means to better perform the task at hand. One may know their job and what is required of them but performing those skills in an environment that is changing and in peril may become more of a challenge. Responders/Rescuers are at both a disadvantage as well as an advantage.

The disadvantage is that countless things are occurring before, during and after they arrive at the scene. It is in essence an unstable environment where emotions are running high. The disadvantage continues as they are entering the unknown. Though they know the basic reason for their presence as the emergency was called in, there are still many unknowns. Has the situation worsened since the initial call? Who else is at the scene? Is it for real? Once on the scene focus and concentration to provide immediate and professional care is upmost but all the while maintain the awareness to remain safe and secure. Even with the best efforts things can get hairy. Even when the patient has been moved for transport things could take a turn and worsen. Again, there are many unknowns. These unknowns can

Rescuer Mindset

each bring a string of issues creating then a multitude of possible outcomes. Situational awareness needs to be in full effect.

The advantages that the Rescuer has is that in most cases they are not alone – either accompanied by several team members or the presence of law enforcement or fire personnel on the scene act as additional eyes, ears, bodies and voices during the event. In these cases situational awareness is a team or group effort. Scene security and safety is a concern and goal of all. It must be shared for order and success to be achieved. Share the responsibility, share the success. Awareness to one another and the respective roles provides needed support in an otherwise stressful and unpredictable atmosphere.

Awareness is enhanced through specialized training methods and exercises which will be discussed in the *Awareness Training* chapter of this text. No out of the ordinary gear or gadgets are required. Each of us possesses the needed tools to hone awareness and become in tuned with our surroundings. Our human sensory systems provide all the resources necessary to sharpen detection and perception for situational awareness.

Sensory Perception Training (S.P.T.)

Sensory Perception Training (S.P.T.) is a must in a self protection doctrine. Being able to see, hear, and feel a situation is imperative to safety, security and survival. Often, hidden in plain sight, things are taken for granted whereas these items may be the keys to a successful or uneventful outcome. Self protection sensory perception is a compound of higher level awareness. This concept will be further discussed in the *Awareness Training* chapter. One level enhances the next but they all work in unison of each, feeding information, alerting and creating necessary responses that offer solutions and most importantly options. Experience itself in the field is the best possible training for anyone. It offers choices and repetitive training scenarios as well as management techniques for stress and practical critical thinking practices.

Time has offered veterans this unique and valuable skill commodity. For those new to the profession, time can be the enemy as they learn the ropes and place themselves in the line of fire, unintentionally or unknowingly. Sensory Perception Training earlier on can help to foster the ability to scan, detected and formulate a scene for safety, giving the capability to be successful.

Rescuer Mindset

Principles of Self Defense

Self defense is a means to respond to an attack or aggressive encounter – it is a means to create a vehicle of escape to safety. Tactics designed to defuse, subdue and/or control an individual or individuals who have become physical is pertinent in the Rescuer/Responders' abilities. Many studies exist showing the need for these sorts of tactics. Statistics define the growing number of professionals who have been to some degree assaulted while attempting to perform their duties. Such is the case that examples of restraint tactics are given based on proposed theory rather than field experience. When Responders are in numbers of two or more, proposed restraining techniques seem valid. But when the Responder is flying solo, these tactics are not so convincing to say the least.

Many relate self defense as a way to fight or having the ability to fight. This is not the case. Self defense is simply that – a defense to protect you to the point you are able to stay safe or make an escape to safety. Choosing to fight with anyone is a no win situation. It is a decision on the part of the participants to lay harm to one another and on themselves. The longer you are in the

Rescuer Mindset

mix, the less chance of survival you give yourself. Anything can happen. The first technique of defense is avoiding it at all costs. The best way to do this is through awareness.

To further grasp the principles of defense, individuals will need to understand the various forms of defense available to them for any given situation. First and foremost is the *mental defense*. This is the response that takes place within each and every person. A decision is made internally, sometimes long before an encounter ever ensues, that creates an attitude of confidence. And this internal confidence is outwardly projected as we make our way through the daily routine, not to be confused with ego, which is often blinded by its own existence to what is around us – actually defeating the purpose of awareness. Ego makes us believe we are better than we are – better than everyone else. Ego convinces us we are infallible and sometimes invincible. It is foolhardy to believe we are indestructible or even close to perfect. To do so suggests we have nothing left to learn, experience or even enjoy. Life and what it has to offer becomes obsolete. In essence we stop growing. Ego, though a means many rely on for daily survival, actually is a sure fire way for limitations to be exposed. And for those in the field limitations can mean the end.

Ego keeps some from ever going outside their comfort zones. And that is where the danger lies – just outside, more-so if not prepared. Elimination of limitation is an extremely valuable resource and why continued research and development is necessary. Ego is not what the individual wants or needs in the defense realm. Instead confidence is what we seek. Know your role and duty as a professional.

Understand why you are there and believe that role has a purpose. And that the role will make a difference. Knowing you have a purpose and that it does matter creates the confidence individuals need to accept their role. It is a role that changes lives, it is a role that saves lives. Be aware that this acceptance can easily become ego and evolve into the popular god like complex. It is through an open mind and heart, the belief that is there is always something more to learn and improve on, meshed with continued training that the ego complex can be tamed.

Mental defense can be 80% or more of the battles we fight – including the ones we fight with ourselves. An inward attitude of confidence projected outward. It is accented in your eyes, in your posture, in the way you sit, stand, walk and talk. That confidence projects in your interaction with others. Others respond well to

Rescuer Mindset

confidence. Confidence begets confidence. Confidence inspires others, motivating them to be better, to be their best. It is a healthy competition of sorts – the more confidence that circulates, the higher the success rate. Team building will be at its highest. Like minds think and act the same. All of this stemming from a mental defense not to allow the cruelty or pettiness of the world to wear you down or get in the way or stop you from moving forward.

Mental defense is mental preparedness – mental readiness. Believe and you shall achieve. The next form of defense is *verbal defense*. It is based on the language – speech and/or body – we use as we interact with others and ourselves. Individuals can often put up walls with just a single word or small gesture – announcing to the world to "back off and leave me alone". This verbal defense lets no one in and usually does not let the individual out. Their world is cut off.

As a professional this makes it extremely difficult to work on a team or in a profession that requires interaction let alone another individual. Others will avoid working with you. This sort of attitude could be linked back to the individual's concept of mental defense and may be a sign of limited confidence on the part of their role or presence in the world in which they live. Beginning there may benefit the execution of verbal defenses.

Verbal Defense – De-escalation

Verbal defenses are the humans' way of interaction with one another. For Responders/Rescuers this is an invaluable tool and yet another skill that can save lives. Initial patient/bystander response may hold the answers to the problem. The more you know, the better you can serve. A negative verbal defense, as described earlier, will only hinder the responder's chances of getting all the facts – this can waste precious time. Engaging the patient and/or bystander in a positive, informative way, regardless of their initial attitude or apprehension to speak with you is monumental. If they are aggressive and you become aggressive, they will only shut down or become more aggressive – now the situation worsens.

A positive verbal defense in the face of verbal hostility is a way to parry the assaults as they come, volleying back with your directive to get the facts. This is in direct relation to the individual's mental readiness – mental defense. It is a process of verbal de–escalation – a positive wearing down process – your attitude towards your role, your belief that you will make a difference, your positive verbal volley to gather the facts to begin

Rescuer Mindset

proper treatment, your prime directive to serve others and perform your duties. Verbal de-escalation is a way to approach a situation that initially appears to be potentially dangerous having the means to turn violent. Verbal de-escalation assists Responders to avoid or reverse the effects of negative confrontation, decrease the intensity and buy additional time. Verbal assaults are often prone to occur as fear plays a major role in the patient or individual causing them to lash out. This lashing out verbally can quickly convert to physically acting out aggressively. Consider the possible outcomes by the words used.

- Do not provoke.
- Attempt to remain calm and non-defensive.
- Keep a safe and secure distance and maintain visual contact with the patient or individual.
- Do not look to reason with the patient but rather be firm and respectful.

Certain situations will be well beyond normal reasoning methods. Define the situation and define the rules – no threats. Avoid getting personal and avoid taking things personal. Don't double team the patient or individual. Only one Rescuer should be the point person while the rest of the team keeps the area safe and secure. A number of incidents can be avoided by verbal – de-escalation techniques.

Body Language

Body language will also play a major part in those initial encounters. Walking on the scene like **you** are the boss puts people on edge and puts up barriers. Air your confidence but do not be brazen with it. Exude your professionalism but do not be condescending. Demonstrate your skills but do not belittle those you assist. As a professional, discernment of a situation can determine the outcome. Maintaining compassion, understanding, concern and attentiveness will be indispensible and helps to engage the human condition. The roles could easily be reversed. You or someone you love could be that patient. How would you respond to someone, called to help, who was not showing you or your problem the proper attention?

Certain actions or movements we may take for granted in our everyday lives might project the wrong message during times of crisis. Crossed arms may suggest disbelief or a threat. Head down or eyes closed may suggest a disinterest or lack of concern. Staring may suggest aggression. Fidgeting may suggest you are in a hurry, impatient or don't care. Be mindful and lead by example.

Rescuer Mindset

Actions and words carry the same weight. Both have the same impact. Both make a difference.

Physical Defense

The next form of defense is always the last resort – *physical defense* – often unprovoked and sometimes unintentional but in all cases always extremely dangerous and violent, regardless of the degree. Violence is violence. Things can quickly and easily get out of hand without the proper training. In a profession where violent acts towards the professional are becoming common place, the need for skills of physical defense would seem a no brainer, but the opposite is true. Though there is an acknowledgement and acceptance on the part of the profession for the need, little is done from the community at large to ensure the safety and ability of the Responder/Rescuer.

Medical procedures and treatment is of course at the top of the professionals' priority list as it should be. But as statistics rise in the numbers of assaults taking place on Responders/Rescuers, the ability to protect themselves in these events is critical and imperative for the survival of the both the professional and the profession.

With physical defense there are two general types: pain compliance and mechanical compliance. Pain compliance is the application of low to moderate pain infliction to the patient by means of a joint manipulation, pressure point or appendage lock to subdue, diffuse and control a physically aggressive situation. Pain compliance tactics work well with patients and/or bystanders who are inhibited by alcohol, certain drugs, sleep deprivation or simply angered.

Mechanical compliance is the application of low to moderate force to key body trigger points that creates movement and states of imbalance in a physically aggressive patient and/or bystander. Such points include the head and neck, elbows and wrists, knees and ankles and hips and waist. Regardless of the patient's state of being, mechanical compliance tactics use body hinge points, movement, mass and gravity against them, helping the Responder to subdue, diffuse and control a situation. By using these body hinge points; particularly the neck, elbows, waist and the knees, Responders will be able to move or position an individual or patient by pushing or manipulating at specific areas of the body that will give way to movement and create imbalance points.

Employing the use of another's energy will assist in eliminating the use of excessive force and power on the part of the

Rescuer Mindset

Responder to restrain and control an aggressive individual. By becoming familiar with body hinge points, Responders will find that these same points can also be used in reverse to lock out the joint or area and used either as a pain compliance or a mechanical compliance tactic. With multiple Responders participating in a restraining process, for overall effectiveness and safety, each can take a position at a major hinge point to control an individual or patient during such an episode.

When employing the use of either pain or mechanical compliance techniques, a basic acquaintance will be needed. A fundamental understanding of their use and application should be grasped to a degree so that the Responder is able to demonstrate and replicate the effects of what the tactics are designed to be and do. Otherwise their use will be useless. Many pain compliance techniques such as joint locks and manipulations are also mechanical compliance techniques as well. In the event such tactics are required, Responders should begin with pain compliance to assess their effectiveness on the individual or patient. If the patient does not respond – flinch, wince, pull away, drop to the ground, yelp, groan, then the pain compliance technique needs to be quickly converted into a mechanical compliance procedure.

Application of pain compliance tactics should always be directed back, in a small circular motion, at the individual the Responder is trying to restrain. Mechanical compliance tactics will often employ a larger motion either linear or circular or a combination of both to create its effectiveness. For the best results using both tactics in succession with each other will be most beneficial for a multitude of situations.

Regardless of which tactic is engaged and working, the Responder's position is very important. When operating with pain compliance techniques, the Responder should be at a 45° degree angle to the individual or patient with the controlled area positioned within the Responder's center and shoulder width. This angle assists in the execution of the pain compliance tactic as well as cutting off the individual or patient's ability to utilize all of their natural weapons; opposite arm, leg and hip. With mechanical compliance movements, the Responder should look to continually move to the side or behind the aggressive subject to keep the advantage while staying out of the direct line of sight of the individual or patient. Instruction by a qualified person in the

Rescuer Mindset

use and application of pain and mechanical compliance tactics should be researched and adapted to every department. As well as ample time devoted in their proper use and function as relatable to the profession.

Current State of Affairs

Current statistical solutions to the growing problem provide explanation and demonstration of techniques used to control such situations, usually involving the use of three or more Responders to carry out the technique. In a perfect world these solutions would be spot on. However, many professionals operate two or less per call. Here is where a gap exists. How does a solo Responder keep the edge?

It should go without stating, when possible, approach all situations with back up. Two or more responders level the playing field and increase the chances of success. There is strength in numbers. Numbers alone could prevent a potentially physical outbreak. But since this is not always the case, if other team members are occupied or not present, Responders/Rescuers require additional skills and training to handle these sort of "on site" emergencies solo. They are already equipped with the necessary skills for emergency medical treatment, they should also be armed with techniques and tactics to protect and defend themselves accordingly in such an event.

Empty handed tactics such as pain and mechanical compliance techniques will give them the edge for assurance and reassurance. Knowing the techniques alone is not enough. Being able to execute the techniques effectively and efficiently is vital to their worth and usefulness, especially when needed. Without that, they are just textbook statistics. Statistics only create more debate and with debate, losing sight of the real problem becomes inevitable. Nothing gets done. Consider who suffers.

Skills such as CPR, First Aid and other federal, state and local certifications require periodic retesting, so should the tactics and knowledge to handle physical aggression, the medically incompetent and those in need, be given the same priority. Even if tactics are never used in the field, regular explanation and comprehensive testing of the material along with demonstration of its use, should be a part of every Responder/Rescuers' yearly training mandate and regime.

The more it becomes so, the more who will do it, the clearer the message of its relevance and importance will be heard.

Rescuer Mindset

It is better to be safe than sorry. Mind, language and body are your greatest assets. Learn to use them efficiently and effectively.

Aptitude for Training

When does the training end and the reality begin? So many of us want to be where the action is, we want to be the one who saves the day. We want to be the hero. There is a certain rush in knowing who played a hand in something out of the ordinary and that who was me. It is commendable, it is admirable but it is not required and can spell trouble.

Far too often many get side tracked by the glitz and glamour of what may be perceived as excitement and adventure. Our perception of what is exciting has been unfortunately molded and painted by television and movies. The glamorizing of almost anything from being an ER doctor to the ups and downs of custodial work is breath taking and awe inspiring. Many rush to a variety of professions for this chance of living and working a life of thrills and spills – only to wind up finding out that there is more down time than depicted and the real excitement does not compete with what they have seen on the small and big screen. What does this leave? Where is the challenge? The challenge then lies within the individual's desire to continue learning and growing through consistent training. This is the reality of many

Rescuer Mindset

professionals. Though there are the periodic moments of *on the edge indulgence*, training is a staple in any qualified and actively participating professional. When does the training end? Never!

The training is what makes the professional a professional. If one is dedicated to the process they will most certainly be dedicated to the job. The attachment to the rush of what is considered to be real will be short-lived and will not sustain engagement let alone a livelihood When things hit bottom so will the interest. It is human nature. It's a hills and valleys approach. Things are great when we are living and riding on top but take a turn for the worst when we live in the valley. It is here when the going gets tough, the tough... usually head for the hills.

Reality has a funny way of changing what we think the rules are and how the game should be played. The reality begins once we are forced to think for ourselves and become responsible for those thoughts and the decisions that are made – the better the training, the better the thoughts, the better the decisions, the better *the professional*. Training keeps you current; training keeps you valid, training keeps you engaged, training keeps you thinking. Training provides a reference point for new ways of thinking and new ways of doing. That is the excitement –

discovering a better way. Lead the way by creating the way. Training will make possible what others neglect to pursue – knowledge. The more you know the more you grow. Know the reality and know the training required.

What is Quality Training?

How can one define it regardless of the context and content? Quality training can only be such if it changes who you are, what you do and how you do it. Regardless of what one does with their life, much of it comes down to the training received. Whether it is from the lessons learned at home growing up, social habits picked up along the way, or work ethics derived from the workplace, training is the foundation. Training forces us to re-evaluate what it is an individual stands for, why the individual does what he or she does and what new heights can be reached. Training is not the end result but rather a milestone one reaches then surpasses on the endless road of learning and growing. Learning and growth is a continuous cycle. There will be many opportunities along the way. It is the responsibility of each of us to seek them out and make every effort to maximize the experience.

Though it must be said that the best training in the world will not make the slightest dent in an individual who is not willing

Rescuer Mindset

to accept, absorb and aspire. Without their consent to be open, it falls unto deaf ears and is kept out by a closed mind. Information passed on is there to enhance and elate as we continue our journey and the search for more. Yet many fall short without even knowing, claiming to have all the answers yet sharing none with anyone including themselves. They become lost within their own beliefs of superiority and ignorance. Pride and ego become personal obstacles that hinder the otherwise opportunity to gain further insight by the experience and efforts of others.

Nevertheless the search goes on. True discoverers keep an eternal beacon, lighting the way not only for themselves but for those who come searching for the same. They light the way for those who will come after. Together these individuals find a way and find each other. Train yourself to see what quality training looks like, sounds like and feels like. See what quality training can do for you. Do not settle. Quality training is not an enigma. It is reality. It does exist and it is most definitely required for those wanting to make a difference, set a standard and change the world. Train hard!

Awareness Training

As mentioned earlier, awareness training is the first step in realizing there is or may be an issue. It is the first step in self protection and self defense. Awareness has more to do with understanding your surroundings than simply seeing what is around you. Of course it is important to visually recognize potentially dangerous situations or individuals but sometimes that may not give you enough time to react properly. Often by the time the mind computes what the eyes are seeing then transmits a response back to the body to do something, precious time could be lost not to mention finding ourselves in an uncompromising or less than favorable position. Looking to expand our senses' sensitivity range will offer an increased awareness state. By broadening our senses we can become in tune with our surroundings on a higher vibrational level – a level that can forewarn us of a circumstance we would want to avoid, internal radar, if you will. All things living or not give off vibrations – energy. In high stressed situations, that energy can become more apparent – certain clues and cues become evident as the event unfolds.

Rescuer Mindset

Further discussion of these clues and cues are covered in the *"Conflict Awareness and Avoidance"* chapter. If we learn to connect with these vibrations/energies we can become more aware of what is around us. As we discussed, Sensory Perception Training (S.P.T.) is a vital component in achieving this enhanced awareness state. It is the backbone of the self protection principles. To develop the deeper perceptions of the senses, each must be honed and drilled with basic exercises. Internal feeling, though not considered one of the five major senses (sight, sound, smell, taste and touch) can provide another level of awareness. Rescuers have a privileged opportunity that gives them a unique perspective into the intimate details of a patient's immediate situation. Their presence on the scene offers them exclusive insight into the initial moments of the patient becoming ill and/or injured. Far before the patient is seen by a medical staff at a nearby hospital, Responders and Rescuers are present from almost the beginning.

These critical and most informative instances can provide the necessary answers to the pertinent questions: *"how did this happen"* and *"why did this happen"*, which will reveal the answer to the question: *"how can I assist"* or *"what can I do."* Emotions are running high and spirits may be low during these critical troubled times. Patients are crying out for help and look to the Responder as a "savior" type figure. Sensory perception for the patient will mostly commonly be heightened but in a way that may not offer a rational and receptive perspective on their part or the parts of those close to them. The Responder's sensory perception will also be overloaded, so much so that the overload may cause the senses to function improperly or in some cases, not at all. This of course, may prevent the Rescuer from properly performing adequate care. Often, during these periods of sensory overload, there is a tendency to overlook or ignore what is directly in front of us.

Past experiences and/or personal beliefs may play a large factor in how we translate these indications. For example, a pregnant woman may not be considered a threat when in fact she is the active shooter in a hostage situation. Our personal experiences with woman who are pregnant may not be that of a killer but more so as someone in need. This can propose a dilemma. Logic will say to us "this cannot be." When in reality it may. Mixed signals are received. Delayed responses can become common place. Making what our experience seems not

Rescuer Mindset

necessarily what is actually happening. This is normal – this is human. Honing the sense of "feeling a situation" may provide additional information as well as alleviate the additional strange put on the common senses during these events.

Consider how many times in life have you said "something just doesn't feel right"? Feeling as though there was something in the air, regardless of how our other senses perceived it? While on the other hand, how many times have you felt "everything was going to be okay"? The connection we share with the world and one another is receptive to the energies that exist. Tap into that and new sight will be given to the remaining five senses.

Sensory Enhancement Exercise (S.E.E.)

To begin, sit comfortably and quietly someplace. You need to be quiet and comfortable not the space or place. Take a few deep breaths and begin to relax and connect. As you breathe deeply in, take in what is all around you – let the five major senses indulge – almost overload. When it begins to become too much begin taking one sense at a time, focus on it, explore it, allow it to reveal things to you. Once you have gone as far as you think is possible, go to the next sense and do the same thing; then the next and so on. There is no order to follow. Pick whichever sense you want to start with. Consider closing your eyes or muffling your ears as you work on the other senses. After sometime, go back to the beginning. Take a few deep breaths and take it all in. This time you should be able to sense your surroundings – feel them.

Feeling your surroundings is simply a collective effort on the part of all your senses working in unison – they are connected so you are connected. Each time you do this exercise you will find that the process of opening up the realms of each sense will be larger and will happen more quickly. Experiment with the experience in different places, at different times of the day, in various moods – however, whenever, wherever. You are training the mind to broaden its reach – you are honing the senses to increase their perception reception.

The above exercise as well as using the technique in daily application does not replace the function or the need to actually using one's senses as designed. Their purpose and their singular abilities are completely necessary. Singular Sensory Sensitivity Awareness (S.S.S.A.) is the ability to use each major human sense as a device to widen the range of self protection.

Sight
Since sight plays a major role in our daily duties, scanning and detecting possible threats or anomalies with the eyes is the

Rescuer Mindset

first step. Regardless of where someone is, a survey of the surroundings, people, places and things, should be ongoing. Many of us tend to get fixed on one point or find ourselves lost in thought that we become inattentive to what is taking place around us. Limitations in sight – tunnel vision – are commonplace. With tunnel vision we now have blind spots in our field of view. This could lead to the possibility of loss, distraction or unwanted issue.

Remaining vigilant to all that is occurring around us will lessen the chances of missing some vital information. With the attentive assistance of your team members the possibilities of missing something are decreased. This should be a commonplace habit for every individual, for every team. The more you do it the better the skill becomes. Everyday, every situation, every moment there is an opportunity to hone this skill. As we are walking take note of who is around you, what they are doing, what they are carrying, how they are dressed, which direction they move. Take note of the area, obstacles in your path, the layout of the land, see your steps before you, mark your path before you take it, know your destination. Watch for people's reactions and interactions – they will often hold clues and cues to intentions, motivations and actions.

Sound

Sound and the use of hearing is also a major alley in the scanning and detecting process. Hearing provides sight to what the eyes cannot physically see. The obvious is to listen attentively, not just hear, to what the patient or those who called for emergency assistance are saying. It's what they are saying and how they are saying it that will provide clarity. For example, if a patient is complaining of massive abdominal pain, listen for the clearness of their voice. Are they gasping for air and responding in a staccato manner as they speak or are they speaking somewhat naturally given the nature or explanation of pain? The assessment of sound, in this case speech, can hold the answers to an actual physical aliment as opposed to a mental one. The patient's personal assessment of the pain differs from their physical presentation.

To broaden the sound sense range, filtering maybe used to pick up what bystanders are saying. What lies in the background or the shadows may be able to be detected by the sounds they make. Filtering provides more than just that, it opens additional doors to self protection and awareness to possible/potential

Rescuer Mindset

conflict. Entering an unfamiliar neighborhood or area may pose a daunting challenge to remain aware even while performing emergency care and treatment. Hearing, again, provides an additional pair of eyes. Listening for what is taking place in the ambience of the situation: gun fire, gathering crowds, emergency back-up, doors slamming, voices, footsteps, cars, sirens, commotion, etc.... These sounds may also be used to distract in a calculated measure. There is a psychological impact that sounds have on an individual. For example, a new born baby who is crying invokes a sense of compassion and care. While a loud explosion or gun fire calls up feelings of fear and terror. It is not uncommon for sound to be used as a method of mayhem causing confusing and diversion. It has been a tactic of war for ages. The attentive alertness of all team members again decreases the possibilities of something going amiss. Sound is yet another tool. And with any tool it needs to be used to be considered useful, otherwise it is just taking up space in the tool box.

Smell

The sense of smell offers us the ability and luxury of distance. Like sight, it is a distance awareness mechanism. Long before we see a building fire, we smell the smoke. Smell can provide particular evidence to an otherwise seemingly quiet occurrence. The detection of gaseous orders such as: mercaptan chemicals used in gasoline and natural gas, ammonia, bleach, mold, mildew and sewage can be direct indicators of the emergency and act as sensory sign posts leading the Rescuer to a proper diagnosis and treatment.

The body itself will give off certain aromas that can identify a condition or illness. Odors that reside in a person's residence can also be clues to certain illnesses and conditions – such as body excrement, urine and flatulence. Though, not a pleasant thing to consider given certain situations, being aware of smells may become a Responder's first line of defense when confronted with an emergency. Often, a pungent smell will come to one's attention first. This awareness can quickly help assess the condition and offer an immediate course of action.

Taste

The sense of taste will most likely not be one a Rescuer will be quick to utilize given the nature of virus, disease and bacteria. But there are certain chemical agents or conditions which give off emissions that will produce a taste, often a sour one. Taste is a chemical property giving us information on the chemical composition of our surroundings. Taste, though, is direct correlation with our abilities to smell. We will often become

Rescuer Mindset

aware of a smell before we are confronted with the taste. Still, if senses have become overloaded by the stress of the event, the smell of a situation may be overlooked. Taste then becomes the next indicator or a thorough assessment.

Touch

Probably one of the most useful senses a Rescuer has is their sense of touch. Given that the profession requires the routine physical examination and assessment of the patient, the sensitivity to what the touch can provide is vital. The tender touch to a patient's limb to determine a fracture or break, the rate of a pulse or the examination of the abdominal region is common practice. It is part of the connection process. Often, the ability to assist in recreating the pain or discomfort is done by touch. Also the ability to console, comfort and alleviate a patient's emotions during these times of stress can be achieved by touch.

Sensitivity and awareness of the sense of touch can provide yet another realm of understanding and a higher level of professional competence that is needed in such sensitive matters. As mentioned earlier, stress inoculation during such events can impair the senses to either a small degree or to a much larger degree causing poor judgment and an altered state of reality.

It is human nature and it is part of our genetic survival gene – fear, fight or flight. Individuals who are faced with these sorts of confrontations do one of three things: freeze, runaway or engage. Regardless of which route taken, the sensory mechanisms begin a process of their own. It is not uncommon to experience one or all of the following: auditory exclusion – selected or muted hearing – ringing in the ear, tunnel vision – limited sight, time perception changes – time seems to either slow down or speed up, speech impediments – loss of voice or stuttering, inability to articulate, memory loss or distortion – what we think may have happened may be different than what had really happened.

Sensory stimuli through exercises and training programs as previously described can greatly enhance both function and focus increasing the ability to remain in control during such stressful episodes. Begin simply by becoming aware of your surroundings, people, places, things and yourself.

Our Choice
Negative aggression is all around us and exists in many forms. This type of energy can easily cloud our alertness and decisiveness. However, you cannot have positive without the negative. At times negative energy seems to swallow up the

Rescuer Mindset

positive energy. It becomes like a snowball – mustering up speed and size as it steamrolls through life. Regardless of its presence and its momentum, we have the choice whether or not to focus on it, play into it, embrace it, feed it or become it. The choice is ours. Not making a choice is giving into it. Accepting it feeds it. Simply rejecting it, even in the smallest way, slows it down, begins to chip away at it and defeats its. Connect with it, but do not become it. Negative aggression can consume you if you allow it.

Awareness allows for options. Singular Sensory Sensitivity and Sensory Perception Training gives you access to those options. Harnessing these basic, built-in human attributes only increases the ability of the professional emergency responder.

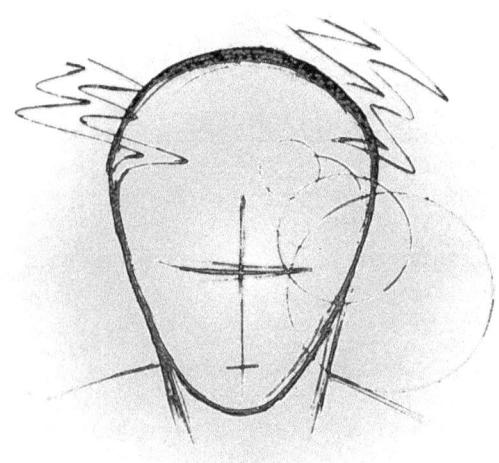

Conflict Awareness and Avoidance

Conflict will always exist as long as there are those who wish to oppose justice and peace. To avoid conflict or better yet be prepared and anticipate it, knowing the basic signs leads to conflict awareness. Some general tell tale signs of an oncoming violent situation include but are not limited to:

- head and/or sight line is lowered
- constant shifting or rapid redistributing of body weight
- rocking back and forth or side to side
- bouncing
- swaying
- a "dead stare"
- wide eyes
- twitching
- hands, fingers, lips, excessive arm movement
- pacing – demonstrating a feeling of being trapped
- clenching of fists or teeth
- nail biting
- tugging of hair

Rescuer Mindset

The above name just a few. These of course are common adrenaline releases leading to a flight or fight response from the individual. It will come down to intent on behalf of the individual and how much of a compromised position they feel they are in which will determine the actual response. The signs may be clearly evident but in some cases they may not be. Proper judgment and discernment is both a practical and indispensable component to the Responder's skill sets and ability to assess situational levels of severity.

Assume that every situation, every patient, every bystander, has the potential to escalate to a violent encounter. This is not to say to become paranoid or distant – this sort of retort will inevitably raise levels of fear and anxiety in the Responder, prohibiting them from performing their duties, accurately and effectively. It is not that everyone sets out to do harm to one another, but the potential is always there, it is always possible. The threat exists. Conflict is as real as it is deadly. It should never be underestimated even in the best of intentions. To know conflict is to recognize it, and in the best cases, before it happens. Know what conflict is, how it feels, how it affects and its effects. Knowing call signs of conflict will help you be aware and assist in avoiding it. Mindset will keep you sharp, keep you focused, keep you professional, keep you safe, and keep you alive.

Now with an awareness to conflict, in order to prevent it we must envision avoiding conflict. Start by visualizing how you want the emergency call to go – using mental imagery. See it happen – play it out – experience the interactions. You create the mindset – you lay out the scenario – a precursor to the actual event. This technique works to eliminate tension, anxiety and creates a workable and successful environment. Mental simulation is a way to give the mind a point of reference. The more often it is done, the more the mind believes it to be real; the more real it seems, the more of what is envisioned will end up in your reality. It is an education and re-education of the mind – the mind is being trained to respond effectively and efficiently.

The mind is stimulated by positive simulation. In the process, the individual is given the chance to see themselves from an observer's point of view while in the midst of performing their duties. The ability exists, in this training technique, to rewind and redo – fix what appears out of place and run the scene again, tweaking as needed – making it perfect. The mind is being trained

Rescuer Mindset

to respond while the individual is being trained to react accordingly. The mind believes it to be real as muscles are programmed and thought patterns are established. These qualities will overflow when confronted with the real thing. Simply by seeing it, presenting our mind with the experience, the Responder will hone methods of practice and response. It is a progression of continuing field training while not in the field.

Visualization

Visualization will play a major role in the development of the Responder's in the field abilities while not in the field. As discussed earlier, mental pictures are created to sustain success, to promote proficiency and expect effectiveness in one's abilities. These mental pictures form a base of stability – a comfort, as well as simulated training scenarios. Visualization is a technique used by top athletes and martial artists, in addition to businessman and corporate giants. Responders can do the same. Visualization is simply a way to enhance or affect the outside world by doing it mentally first – it is a form of positive thinking. Think it, see it, believe it, do it, be it. It then becomes a projected positive outlook or attitude. Visualization is an opportunity to use all the senses thoroughly in a controlled environment. A concentrated focus to

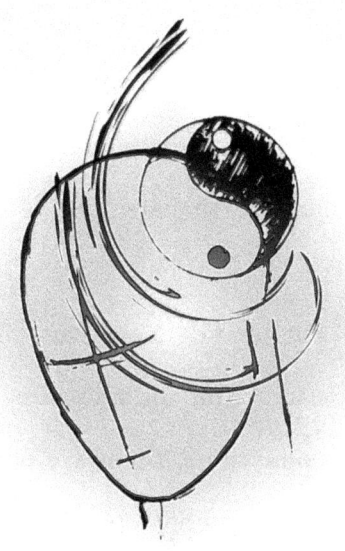

Rescuer Mindset

detail – response behavior – offers the chance to sharpen, research, modify and polish the muscle memory of one's skills.

Visualization is an endless arena of training. Visualization can also be used as a means for problem solving. It will allow for a bird's eye view of the situation – as if taking the part of an observer. The one who is least affected by the stresses of the situation is usually the observer.

Visualization can also have the same effect but in a negative way if thought patterns of failure and inability are the focus. What we think of the most will come to be. Be aware of the possibly of negative infiltration. Self destruction is always a danger. The best intentions and the best efforts can be thwarted by the most basic unconstructive thoughts and beliefs. The notion that a call could go bad is always a risk for any Responder/Rescuer. The potential to over think and focus on the likelihood of its demise can become a thing of habit. It becomes a domino effect that can easily start spinning out of control. Past experiences or situations may have great bearing on how these negative thoughts and beliefs constantly emerge. A hundred calls can be a success but all it takes is one to change our thinking and void the success of our previous achievements.

Proper visualization techniques can help overcome questions of confidence and security – often arising from a distorted self image. It is recommended that individuals who are experiencing an overload of negative thoughts and emotions may wish to seek further assistance in the way of a counseling to discuss alternative methods to surmount these habits of thinking and feeling.

Self Awareness

Of course no one knows for sure how anything will ever play out. The road to hell has been paved with the best intentions. Hell, in this case, does not have to refer to a place of eternal damnation, but more so as a state of outcome to a situation that has gone out of our control. Sometimes we must just accept the things we cannot change and work to better what we can. And what we can always make better is our self. This is the true focus of any individual. To better serve the world we must be able to serve ourselves accordingly. That means knowing when enough is enough, when rest is needed, when a time out is overdue, when it is time to allow others to call the shots.

Self awareness is the best method to avoid conflict – internally and externally. If you are on edge, all that surrounds you, all who interacts with you, will also be on edge. It will be a

Rescuer Mindset

matter of time before the bomb goes off. And who pays the price? Everyone. But who's left holding the bag after the dust settles? You are.

Internally, individually, we are required to check our progress, our current state of being. It is a constant changing state. Otherwise we go unmonitored – unaccountable. And if we are not accountable for ourselves, who will be? Accountability ups the responsibility we entrust ourselves with, for ourselves. No two moments are or will be the same. Just as no two situations will be the same. Self awareness puts into perspective where we are, how we are, and why we are at that or any given moment. Self awareness is an attempt to never be taken off guard. Control the things we can change – ourselves. Make an effort – take responsibility.

The saying *"I'm not my brother's keeper"* is not dismissing the need, duty or intent to be of service to others but rather it is stating that being in the service of others is in direct relation to the individual – the one in service – acting reasonably, responsibly and rationally, thus, being in service to yourself first. We are our own keeper. We cannot rely on others for this duty. The word "keeper" used in the original Hebrew translation of the passage from the book of Genesis actually means "master". With further contemplation brings to mind the Asian proverb that *"true mastery is not mastery of others but of one's self."* Again, pointing directly back to the individual. We are our own masters – we are the keepers of self. These profound interpretations reiterate the importance and the necessity of self awareness. How will we know where we are going if we do not know where we have been? How will we know what we will become if we do not know who we are?

Rescuer Mindset

Conflict Resolution

Conflict resolution is simply the ability to resolve conflict. The definition is easier said than done. Conflict comes in many shapes and sizes and it also comes in many forms and from various sources. Conflict can be easily recognized in, with and by others, but often it is overlooked when it is from within. Often we will find that the conflicts we hold within will, at times or quite regularly, spill out and over into our daily living. Our conflict now becomes that of others. We make our problems a problem for others, merely because of our inability to control and resolve.

Conflict resolution, as with anything, starts with awareness – knowing it exists, seeing its signs, taking the steps to resolve it, being honest – knowing is more than half the battle. We will find that in most cases conflict will hit us head on. The "in your face" approach to conflict is part of its design to disturb and take control by off-setting our current position – it quickly puts the receiver on edge or even worse, shuts them down – allowing conflict to take over and dominate. Conflict feeds itself by breeding confusion and disorder. The more of each, the more conflict will dominate. But there are options. The following will

Rescuer Mindset

cover some general approaches to conflict management and resolution.

Understand that conflict itself is an unpredictable, unstable entity often with a mind of its own. There is no telling how far someone or something will go once conflict takes hold. Your job during the presence of conflict is to effectively and efficiently de-escalate the potential of it becoming violent. Being prepared is an adage of continuous self protection.

Give Way

Allow the conflict a passage – space to proceed. There will be cases when conflict is merely just an opportunity for another to vent or release some pent up discontent. Having the opportunity to liberate that discomfort may pose to be a simple yet effective way to de-escalate a situation. As a Responder/Rescuer, patient's emotions may be running, or they may be basically scared. Giving way may afford them enough freedom to return to "normal".

Change Direction

Changing direction is the beginnings of actively engaging in conflict on a more involved level. By changing direction, we look to reorient or change the course of the conflict. When giving way does not appear to be enough, looking to alter the flow of the conflict will sometimes offer a subtle alternative to the regaining of order. Changing direction could entail verbally responding in a gentle, monotone voice, taking the time to see the situation as the patient or person experiencing conflict sees or views it. This is comparable to doing the opposite of what is actually taking place; similar to the reverse psychology approach – leading – where the Responder makes gestures or gives cues or commands for the patient to follow.

Changing direction could also simply be a matter of changing your present course of action to something entirely different such as allowing a co-Responder to intervene. Changing direction will offer a variety of options as long as the professional stays alert and calm.

Diffuse

Diffusing an escalating conflict situation is paramount for the utter safety and success of the Responder/Rescuer. Diffusing is the act of dissipating something over a larger area. As things begin to heat up, adding fuel to the fire will just not help but worsen matters. Diffusing is a matter of simultaneously using the giving way and changing direction principles, cycling through each repeatedly as a means to disseminate the conflict – weakening its power and lessening its stronghold.

Rescuer Mindset

Diffusing can also take the form of physical presence where as the number of Responders/Rescuers, EMS, Police, etc., at the scene, can greatly reduce the chances of conflict arising. It creates an order or balance that could deter any possible prospect of threat. Diffusing will rely on vigilance and perseverance to accomplish its goal.

Modify and Adapt

Just as it is stated, certain situations will require modification and adaptation. Conflict is a changing environment and since no one knows which direction it will take, it is a matter of being on top of the situation. Modifying is a way to make something less extreme or to change the nature, structure or intent of something. Adapting is making the current situation suitable or adjusting it to meet the need. Coupled together, modify and adapt offer the professional alternatives. This helps to roll with the punches without being rolled over by the punches. Like in boxing, they are mental forms of bobbing and weaving, ducking and dodging, blocking and parrying.

Each conflict as with each encounter will be unique. As things unfold, keeping the edge is a matter of staying sharp and focused at to what is actually transpiring. Being aware of your own mental and emotional state as well as taking into account the mental, emotional and possibly physical state of the patient, will keep the doors of modification and adaptation wide open.

Go With It

Going with it relates to the concept of push and pull. The common response when pushed is to push back, as the common response to being pulled is to pull back. These often instinctive reactions tend to create a tug-of-war scenario, sometimes even a stalemate, where there is no room to give way. The opposite of the instinctual reaction to the aforementioned is actually the best course of action – when pulled, push; when pushed, pull. You now find yourself "going with it".

Going with it permits the individual to be or remain in effect or operation without altering their condition – it does not put you at a disadvantage. There is a displacement, but it is a mutually accepted decision on both sides to partake in the engagement – the two are moving in the same direction, covering the same ground regardless of point of view. And as the one – the Responder – on the receiving side of the conflict, going with it helps to maintain distance, position and momentum. Often, it will be found that the momentum created by the push or pull and mutually accepted by the Responder, will be enhanced towards the favor of the Responder. Your acceptance will give you the edge

Rescuer Mindset

since most aggression/conflict does not expect a reaction or response other than cowering and defeat. Simply don't allow this to take place.

Get Out of the Way

To avoid a freight train from hitting you, what are your options? Common sense would tell you that the only real option is to get out of its way – and fast! Dealing with major conflict can be looked at in the same manner – don't block or impede its way. Yet, far too habitually, many will choose to meet it head on, sometimes even with the overwhelming odds of success not in their favor. This may be a good strategy for playing Monopoly or even a night in Vegas, depending on how deep your pockets are, but as an emergency professional, toying with time and lives is never a safe bet. Getting out of the way is just letting the conflict pass. It is realizing that something is more than you can handle and either backup or a serious reassessment of the situation is drastically needed before things really go south – for any and all involved.

Responders may be required to deal with multiply dilemmas, making a judgment call on which or who takes priority may be greatly influenced by the freight train analogy of conflict resolution. Standing in the line of fire or not asking for assistance is not a prerequisite of being a hero or heroine. The choice to perform your duties as a professional has afforded you a *hero to humanity* title and it is best served alive and intact.

Conflict will steamroll you if it is allowed to do so. Getting out of the way and letting it pass affords the luxury of time – maybe not a lot, maybe just enough to come at it from a different way, maybe even to temporarily derail it or slow it down, but time nonetheless. The second go at it might prove to be more successful and the previous methods of conflict resolution may be employed in their use and capability to assist the situation until further aid is acquired. Getting out of the way creates space and space creates time and distance – giving the Responder distance to regroup and time to reassess.

Conflict is NOT equal, though this is not a method to resolve conflict; it is worth conveying that all conflict, however similar, is not at all equal. If that were the case, there would only be need for one method or tactic to quickly resolve it. Yet, conflict comes in many forms and ranges. On the flip side, conflict does not discriminate. It shares its iniquity equally. It comes from all walks of life. No one is immune to being either consumed by conflict or being on the receiving end of it. Centuries of history

Rescuer Mindset

has demonstrated that we are a race that has resolved to resolve things with conflict. Almost to say that conflict is human nature even for those who seek to avoid it.

Conflict is but a turn of the corner or the uttering of a syllable or two away from rearing its ugly head. Add a bit of tension, a touch of confusion and top it off with a possible medical emergency, not to mention the possible additional inclusion of illegal substances, alcohol and the occasional human stupidity factor, conflict is a time bomb ready to blow. Here lies the paradox: even looking to avoid conflict, it still exists ☐ it still breeds, waiting to be released at the most inopportune moments of our lives, regardless of our intent.

Since conflict is not equal, so also is how conflict is viewed by others. You may consider conflict an inconvenience, something that gets in the way and halts progress, stifles goodwill and makes the worst out of the best. But someone else may find supremacy and gratification in conflict. The old saying "misery loves company" is not a far cry to believe that conflict exists for the satisfaction of some. Used as a means or weapon to "get what they want", conflict proves to be a formidable ally and tactic. For them it simply works.

As a Responder/Rescuer, your vocation is a hot bed for the potential outbreak of the more than occasional conflicted condition. It is a high stressed field of profession, both for you and the patient. The gist is not to be naïve with regards to conflict – to its signs and its effects.

Connect

Sometimes and for some, conflict may be a cry for help or attention. It is a way for others to connect, to fill a void or to reach out with the hopes of ridding their lives of loneliness, emptiness or fear. Having someone present, such as a Responder/Rescuer, who is available to be attentive to their needs could in itself be a life saving measure. Consider, for a moment, the possibilities of the power of interaction – the power of connection – compassionate vigilance.

Connection creates a balance in an otherwise unbalanced condition – long or short term. The Responder's presence brings assurance and reassurance. Their cry for help has been championed. The time spent, with just someone to listen and to pay attention, offers hope and encouragement that things can get better. Sadly, the use of emergency services for non-medical emergency use is taxation on the system, a misuse of resources and imposes on the needs of those who are in serious difficulty.

Rescuer Mindset

However, turning a blind eye to a call for help goes against basic human ethics.

The powers of discernment and sensitivity can offer the needed "void fill" for the patient while operating in a clear and concise way so as not to deplete the system further. Simply, a gesture of compassion, on the part of the Responder, conveys a feeling of hope, on the part of the patient, that they are not alone. Though medical emergency services were not performed in cases such as these, matters of the heart were addressed and potentially resolved. Consider how to resolve conflict in you and with others.

As mentioned earlier, conflict resides everywhere and regrettably, in everyone. Accepting that will help alleviate and release much of the stress retained by and associated with the thoughts or feelings of conflict. Become aware of your personal signs of conflict – what are your personal paradigms, prejudices and triggers? Do you bring on conflict in yourself by the thoughts you have, the words you use, the actions you take? Do you think before you act or speak or are you a siren chaser? Do you secretly or openly blame others for your shortcomings or stumbles in life?

Do you take responsibility, completely, for you? Or do you rely on others to pick up the pieces and clean up the messes?

How you treat yourself, how you think of yourself, how you talk to yourself and speak of yourself will determine how you do so with others. Much of what we do to others stems from how we do unto ourselves. If we lack self respect then we will not be able to respect others properly. If we physically abuse our bodies; drugs, alcohol, food, negative forms of pain or punishment, then we will treat others with the same lack of compassion and care as we do with ourselves. "Do unto others as you would have done unto you" starts with how you treat yourself.

The Japanese phrase *masakatsu agastsu* – true victory is self victory, sums up the need to control one's self before making any attempts to control another. If you are out of balance, no situation you encounter will ever be balanced, no matter how hard you try.

Consider space and position – yours and others
Each one of us has personal space. There is a defined boundary that exists. And for each one of us that personal space is different. Some like up close and personal – others do not. Some prefer an arm's length distance while some require a lot

Rescuer Mindset

more. Consider your own personal space. How does it make you feel when someone breaks that barrier? On edge maybe?

Whether they are aware of it or not, when our boundaries are breached, most of us become uncomfortable. Keep in mind that the personal space of someone who may be experiencing some sort of medical emergency can quickly become even smaller than normal. Diving right in, though seeming like the compulsory protocol, may incite a form of conflict that could prevent the proper providing of needed care. Illness, discomfort and even fear often limit tolerance levels. That tolerance can be put to the test by the slightest touch, the purest gesture or even the kindest word – all can easily be misinterpreted in times of crisis. Regardless of the Responder's intent to provide necessary and responsible care, a conflict has now ensued.

An assessment of space and position is in order to avoid any unnecessary obstacles that could prevent you from performing your duties. Simply approach the patient slowly and with reverence as you enter their space – their personal space. Inform them that your treatment and care may require questioning and them to be touched in order to diagnose and care for their condition. If possible, if coherent, obtain a verbal consent. If not, obtain verbal consent from a spouse, guardian, family member, friend, and caregiver – whoever may be present. This is a good habit to get into and demonstrates your respect for the patient and regardless of their condition still requires and deserves the courtesy owed to all human beings.

Considering your own space and position is a continuing effort to maintain personal safety and protection. Care should always be taken as to your proximity to a possible violent or erratic patient as well as to those who are present at the scene. Maintaining a clear view of the area, its contents, its occupants, your comrades and most importantly your exit and/or escape routes, keeps from experiencing "tunnel vision". Working with your team members to secure and monitor a scene can prevent unwanted surprises.

Don't allow yourself to be or get boxed in.
Refrain from being overly or needlessly engaged or distracted by the commotion that regularly offsets the productivity of the task. Space and position can easily become compromised if focus is lost not to mention valuable time and attention being taken away from the patient by minute diversions. Personal space and position of a Responder should clearly not be violated in such a way as to prevent emergency medical care.

Rescuer Mindset

Regular communication between team members regarding Responder well being and environment security should be maintained throughout the rescue. A practice of well defined safety measures and precautions should be set in place for all active Responders/Rescuers at all times.

It must also be taken into account that religious, cultural, lifestyle and even social consciousness is indeed a concern and consideration when referring to space and position of those who you serve. Language barriers would offer some troublesome terrain, if you are not able to effectively communicate. Cultural differences may dictate that women and men function on separate and specific levels. This may pose the need for alternative ways to make contact, acquire cooperation and to achieve success. Lifestyle and/or social diversities may conjure up discomfort, prejudice, supremacy and even hatred on the part of the patient, victim, bystander(s) and even the Rescuer that may greatly encumber their performance and/or willingness to cooperate or accept aid. It would be beneficial for Responders to be educated on the areas they serve. This foreknowledge can provide a plan of action for effective response tactics in case such an event unfolds. Keep informed, stay informed, always be informed.

Become aware

Though awareness has already been mentioned and discussed in this text, repeating its relevance and importance is always necessary. As with anything, once something becomes natural and instinctive, awareness levels decrease because the comfort levels increase. The balance is to maintain both the comfort levels of your skills and awareness levels of safety and security. As team members and as individuals, training is the key. Knowing is more than half the battle. Knowing is knowledge and knowledge is success. Awareness is yet another tool that enhances your performance as a professional emergency responder. Conflict resolution may require conflict to resolve the problem.

Unfortunately, as the world would seem to have it, conflict is not in short supply and does not seem to be going the way of fast lived fads or trends of the day. Conflict is very real and always looms about. With that in mind, the consideration that to resolve conflict in its most horrific forms may sadly require an equal or greater form of conflict in return. When a situation has become physically aggressive and/or violent, regardless of the degree, certain measures will be needed, and certain actions will

Rescuer Mindset

be required. At the end of the day, a Responder's safety, security and life take precedence to all else.

What is being addressed is that point within an encounter where verbal communication has halted, reasoning has ceased and escape is now compromised – the safety and/or life of the Responder is now in jeopardy. A physical episode has now ensued. Survival and escape is the prime directive. Since a Responder/Rescuers' ability to protect and defend themselves varies from region to region, it is necessary to be advised on your rights and allowances in such cases in regards to your area's stand and take on these types of matter. But as stated before, at the end of the day the safety and life of the Responder takes priority. Self preservation in the face of danger is a basic human right and privilege. And as public servants, these rights and privileges should always be respected and never in question. It is the sole responsibility of the Responder to act accordingly and this may include the use of self defense as an act of being responsible.

Regular discussions and forums should be offered to assist Responders/Rescuers with their education, understanding and awareness of procedure as well as the skills to manage such encounters. This not only includes just the physical encounters but includes attitudes, emotions and adjustments that occur in the wake of such experiences. Mental and emotional rehabilitation, as well as the possible physical rehabilitation is required to assist an individual back to a confident and dignified state of being. Effects of such encounters can be life altering even if the event was classified as a minor physical altercation. Human intensity levels run high and one's reality can be shattered. Follow up in the way of assessment, counseling, reassurance, and encouragement to help regain the individual's own security and self assurance may be needed. Team building classes and projects will create a support network so no one ever feels alone.

Rescuer Mindset

Application

Theory is just one piece of the puzzle and can often cause the individual to get trapped in text book methods, statistical explanations and presumed and assumed concepts. Theory is but a tool to develop direction and means of outlining a process. It is a necessary step but it is not the end. Application is the next step – applying those theories and methods to what really exists. Application involves putting theory into motion – taking what we have learned, training it and setting it to muscle memory. Application is the environment to work out the kinks and remove the bugs from the system. Application brings to light what is useable and what are just words. Words enlighten and inspire but application provides stability and framework that functions when it is needed and when it counts. Application becomes the reality.

Move, Connect, Control

Rather than fight for your position, take your position. Fighting begets fighting. Fighting consumes resources and depletes needed time and energy very quickly. Fighting opens up too much opportunity for the tables to be turned on the Rescuer/Responder. First priority is immediate personal safety –

Rescuer Mindset

without that – the Rescuer/Responder will not be able to perform their necessary function and role.

Distinction, Retention, Response

Through a series of basic movements, Rescuers/Responders can be taught simple responses for a multitude of physical encounter situations. Terms such as basic and simple are used not to denote these tactics are elementary in their effectiveness but rather to stress the need for the executable ease of their efficiency. In times of distress, complicated, fine motor-skilled movements will be difficult and often require a thought process. The stress causes suppression of the frontal brain activity as our adrenaline is dumped. The importance of executing simplistic gross motor skills will be most beneficial and less time consuming hence expelling far less of our physical and mental energy – trainable and retainable. The fewer chances of getting stuck, confused or overwhelmed during an encounter will greatly increase the prime directive to provide emergency care and or treatment.

When beginning working with new material, for it to be understandable, functional and responsive, repetitive practice through the use of drills needs to occur from the start. Partners will be inclined to fight, resist and test the material. Initially, however, partners should cooperatively assist one another by allowing the techniques to work. Both participants learn what is taking place and what it feels like to play both roles while experiencing what is happening during a specific encounter. This provides a deeper understanding into the mechanics and the ideology behind the encounter/defense scenario. During these initial cooperative training encounters participants get familiar with reaction, position, body alignment and displacement, movement, space, time and control – all in a manner that builds a foundation of usable base responses. This makes what is learned distinctive and retainable. The next stage of development would be to add low to moderate resistance to the encounter practice scenario. Small doses of cooperative resistance will enhance the threat as well as the response time and physical reaction – becoming instinctive. Gradually the resistance is increased – continually building the learned responsive reaction one level at a time. We want reaction not action. Action requires thinking, processing and doing – this requires precious time. Whereas reaction requires doing – thinking and processing are eliminated because a learned responsive reaction has been taught making it instinctive. After some time a pattern of responsive reactions are

Rescuer Mindset

cataloged and quickly recalled for when needed. Recognition and recollecting will quickly find familiar positions and situations – making them now retainable and usable.

Keep in mind that as the resistance is increased so is the overall intensity of the responsive reaction. Though some may feel this is reality based training, it will also increase the chance of injury infliction for the participants. This only defeats the purpose of the training and in turn puts professionals on the injured reserve list. Training should always be done with the overall safety and concern of each partner. We are all players on the same team. The well being of each to return to the field to perform is paramount. To intentionally, carelessly or accidentally injure a colleague for the sake of training or as a means to prove something is unacceptable. Accidents will happen, but with a conscious effort to maintain safety and respect, they will be far and few between.

The goal is to build a solid base of trainable, retainable and usable responsive reactions. Quantity is not important. The quality of their usefulness – effectiveness and efficiency – is what the practitioner is after. The techniques one acquires should be able to be executed in a multiple of positions and scenarios:

standing, against a wall, in a crowded area, on the ground. This makes them truly functional and usable rather than *situationally specific* – having limited or exclusive uses. But rather, techniques that are *situationally diverse* – meaning multiple applications – without limitations – is what should be sought. Though each encounter is unique, our learned responsive reactions will ensure the taking of position required to gain or regain control of the situation. This responsive reaction replaces the instinct to fight for the position, which can create too many variables and leaves only two options: hold your position or fight some more.

The more variables, the more time expires and the more the chance of success begins to diminish. Eliminate the negatives and accentuate the positives of the training. In a short time – a workshop, a series of classes, a one or two day seminar – these learned responsive reactions can be ingrained by following the prescribed method of Repetitive Cooperative Resistance Training (R.C.R.T). Through high, non-resistive repetitive drilling, participants can acquire the fundamental skill set needed giving them the protective/defensive edge. High repetition is the key ingredient in retention. Keeping movements/responses simple and direct will create ease of execution with this repetitive

Rescuer Mindset

retention drill. Rapidly, reactions will become natural responses – mentally and physically.

SECTION V - PREVENTIVE MEASURES

> *Parent's View…*
>
> *…Where are they? It seems like it's been an hour since we called 911 and they're not here yet… Oh thank God, finally they're here. But why are they taking so long to get out of the ambulance? Don't they realize my child needs help, like now! What are they doing? …We are the ones in need here, so why are they being so rude? It's as if they don't want to hear what we've got to say… I might not be a doctor but I know my child…*

Rescuer Mindset

Stress Reduction - Clean Up Your Own House First

Leadership activities should be focused at detecting sources of organizational stress. Healthcare and public safety are all unbalanced occupations with disproportionate levels of downtime versus short intervals of high stress activity. Having identified many sources of stress in earlier sections of this book, the organizational responsibility towards stress reduction should be aimed at cultural behavior modification training that would lead to the change in the prevalence of stress stimuli.

Stress is a public health-type problem which is centered on behavior and behavior modification. We illustrated that point easily with the discussion of stress-related sugar addiction and its multiple relationships with chronic illness. Stress can be immediately addressed with medication, but medications do not remove, reduce or mitigate the cumulative or incident-related effects of stress. Medications are an individual intervention and not one at a public health level. Some stress factors are inherent to the occupation and are acceptable to emergency workers if they are educated and conditioned to mitigate their effects. Workplace climate surveys are good ways of assessing workplace wellness and stress. These surveys allow leaders to adjust workplace conditions and practices to reduce adverse actions related to stress.

Once the workplace climate has been assessed, actions such as job redesign or initiatives focused on leadership can be designed. One of the major complaints listed in EMS and healthcare job satisfaction studies was the perceived lack of respect by leadership of emergency workers in the field. Simple leadership skills education and personal awareness training can help mitigate the development of adversarial relationships between emergency workers and management. Another effective tool for mitigating negative relationships is cross-cultural communication training for both leaders and emergency workers alike.

Community Building

Social support networks represent the proverbial "double-edged sword" whereas inadequate or inappropriate social support may also make emergency workers more susceptible to develop PTSD. In studies of police officers specifically, it was discovered that those who communicated with their peers or supervisors may actually have increased likelihood to experience increased stress syndromes. Considering this point, it should be noted that support networks should be well developed and not necessarily ad hoc, as non-coping networks could exacerbate negative consequences of stress. It is also important that support networks are not forced upon the emergency worker in order to meet corporate SOP's or demands.

The irony of emergency worker support networks is centered in the individual. Despite the apparent need for a social support network, the typical coping mechanism of emotional distancing will most likely dissuade veteran emergency workers from seeking appropriate means of social support. As such, the slippery slope of cumulative stress syndromes continues as low social support may likely lead to increased stress symptomatology as well as increased perceptions of organizational stress, and ultimately…burnout. Again, support mechanisms and networks should not be forced upon the emergency worker.

Regarding social support and consequences, British EMS participants in a mental health study who took mental health medical leave reported low perceptions of family support. Possibly in agreement with the aforementioned discussion of negative aspects of non-coping social support, the same

Rescuer Mindset

participants reported there was no significant difference in their perceptions of peer or organizational support. This last point may suggest that the primary social network being most effective for the mitigation of long-term or cumulative negative stress syndromes would be the family support structure. This assumption has been investigated an implemented into the military traumatic brain injury (TBI) education program for returning war veterans and their families. Caution must be taken with these considerations, as it has been previously discussed that there are chronic adverse effects transferable to family members through repeated exposure to third party accounts of job-related stress.

CISM/CISD and War Stories

In the emergency worker community, one of the most widely used forms of response to rescuer stress particularly PTSD is the critical incident stress debriefing (CISD) or critical incident stress management (CISM) counseling. The processes involved in (CISD), although well thought out may actually exacerbate anxiety and actually be ineffective. In the incident-related stress casualty, the re-enactment or revisualization of traumatic experiences has been considered a causal factor in the delay of the psychological healing process and therefore in involuntary imposition of CISD/CISM may actually yield detrimental effects. Considering this statement, primary actions focused at mitigation of the cumulative effects of organizational stress should be considered early, and efforts focused at developing worker resiliency through wellness education and programs should be adopted. If employed, a long-term program for post-traumatic stress surveillance should be utilized rather than imposition of mandatory debriefings done on short-term basis.

We've all heard them; they usually start with "No shit, there I was!" "War stories" typically begin at the most inopportune or unexpected times. They present during intervals of personal healing and dropped "guards" which are parts of the normal coping processes. The telling of "war stories" represents healthy expressions of psychological stress. It is the gradual release of pressure at the time determined by the emergency worker. The healthful benefits of story-telling are exhibited over long-periods of time as the individual subconsciously finds a way to come to terms with their experience.

To the leader, co-worker, friend or family member who is listening, they then represent the positive social network needed

Rescuer Mindset

to aid in the healing process of the stress casualty. There is no need for the listener to acknowledge or justify in any way the feelings of the emergency worker as the story is being told, but rather just to listen as a genuinely concerned recipient of this vital information about the worker's life. Stories may include accounts of "what I could have done" or "what I should have done" or they may illustrate feelings of guilt such as "why couldn't it have been me?" Regardless of the nature of the story, it is important to allow the process to continue and to acknowledge that the feelings expressed are normal reactions and not those of weakness or inability to cope.

In the wake of the events of 9/11, public outcry for rescuer support and assistance led to an influx of forced CIS debriefings, which in retrospect may not have been conducive to emergency worker healing, but rather it may have served to quell the anguish of public onlookers who wanted to help. In the future rather than force procedure upon our peers, we should consider the normal healing processes involved with cumulative and incident-related stress. The next time someone wants to tell you a war story, take heed that they have bestowed upon you a great trust as they could be reaching out to you as their positive social network.

Inspired by the painting "The Angel at the Empty Tomb"
by Bartolomeo Schedoni 1613

Rescuer Mindset

Physical Well Being

It should go without saying that the need to be physically fit, not only to perform one's duties in the field in a manner that does not over stress or tax the body but for the overall quality and longevity of life, is a must for everyone. Physical health and well being benefits everything: mood, thinking, breathing, appearance, strength, awareness, increases energy levels, battles fatigue, and improves sleep just to name a few. Countless information exists supporting the benefits – internally and externally. We have all heard it, many of us have read it but still far too few do it or make the effort. Physical health and well being is actively taking full responsibility of your person. It demonstrates your care and commitment to you. No one else can do it for you.

Fitness is a simple equation: some is better than none and more consistency is better than some once in awhile. Consistency, as with anything, is the key to success. Fitness is a lifelong pursuit and should be a part of one's daily routine. It is a choice. Often, people will create a picture of fitness that resembles a professional or Olympic athlete. Images of long, high intensity workouts overrun the mind and can keep people from ever starting – they believe it to be too much work. If not an

Rescuer Mindset

athlete, why train like one? But fitness does not have to be a job in itself. Yes, it takes time and effort but fitness has to be a personal thing. You have to want to be fit and healthy. If you have that, you have what it takes.

"Some is better than none" offers that whatever we choose to do will have it benefits. We just need to choose something and stick with it. Health is a matter of life or death – there is a choice and here is where it lies. If given any other circumstance or situation, most, if not all, would choose life. Health is one of those times. As with any piece of equipment or technology used in your industry or profession, your body and its well being is not any different. It needs to be cleaned, checked, and maintained regularly. It needs to be fueled, strengthen, recalibrated, enhanced and super–charged. It needs to be tested, educated, improved and made aware. Physical well being goes back to personal protection and awareness. Good awareness starts with self awareness. Be aware of yourself in your environment. If not, you can be caught off guard. And being caught off guard is never a good thing, after the fact is just too late.

Diet

Health starts with what you put in – you are what you eat. Food is our source of nutrients and fuel. It is also the source of our world's health issues. More is better and fast is easy. Food choices are made simple for us by offering what is convenient and not what is necessarily good for us. Thinking about what we eat, how we eat, when we eat and where we eat has been left to big corporations and advertisers. We simply just do not think about it or consider what it is doing to us. Only after health problems such as weight gain, digestive issues, irritable bowel syndrome, and blood sugar or blood pressure concerns arise, do we choose to do something. Why wait until then? The time is now and today is the day.

Using food as an example, our society struggles with the notions of restriction and deprivation from the things we like. It is an all or nothing mentality, win or lose, black or white – there is no in between. Setting the bar to these points makes it impossible for anyone to succeed let alone want to try. Rather than restrict, make it a habit to limit the amounts. Less is more and simple is success. Restriction most likely will lead to wanting something more. We all want what we can't have and find we will go to great lengths to get it. Create a less is more mindset for your personal

Rescuer Mindset

health and well being. Limit the intake of less than healthy food choices. The less you intake the more your health will improve.

Exercise for some is like the sound of finger nails screeching on a chalk board. Chills go down the back as their hair stands on ends. But it doesn't need to be that way. Again, fitness is an individual thing. Make it personal. If you don't like free weights, use body weight resistance exercises like varieties of push-ups, pull ups, pike press, abdominal and core movements. If you don't care for running; try bike riding, walking or a form of aerobics. If you have joint issues or contend with injures; work with elastic bands, seat exercises or Tai Chi. If you're looking for something more intense; try kettle bells, plyometrics, a martial art like Aikido, cross training or circuit training. If you're looking for something more serene but beneficial; explore yoga, Pilates or flexibility classes. Need motivation and direction? Try group fitness classes, workout with a buddy or schedule one-on-one personal training. There are countless options and outlets for anyone and everyone to be personally fit. A well maintained body is a well maintained mind.

Give yourself a reason to be healthy and fit. If you can't do it for yourself, do it for someone else: your spouse, girlfriend or significant other, do it for your kids, your parents, family and friends, do it for your pets, your job or hobby. Do it for your car! Do it for something but just do it. For every excuse you give yourself there are countless reasons to rebut that excuse. The energy put into excuses could just as easily be put into becoming fit and staying fit.

Being fit does not mean you are the next Ironman or Olympic Gold Medalist. Being fit is being able to move through your day and daily regimen without discomfort and overload, such as: going up and down a flight of stairs, walking short or long distances, breathing, tying your shoes, comfortably wearing your clothes or uniform, picking something up, performing the duties of your occupation and enjoying time with your family and friends. Life offers enough obstacles each day for many to contend with, compounding that with less than favorable health practices is only adding fuel to the fire. Healthy living is a choice and it is a proactive decision to live better and be better.

Make good habits part of your lifestyle. Not all at once but a little at a time – don't overload – take one step at a time. Success is achieved this way. Step–by–step also provides the chance to modify and tweak as needed. You see and feel progress

Rescuer Mindset

– it is monitored intelligently. Adding as you begin to see and feel improvement. As you improve, your body will want to take on more of a challenge – give it the challenge. It would be simple to include in this text a series of exercises and workout routines for the reader to perform. But this would only serve to offer just one option and an option based solely on the author's preferences and experience. Fitness is individual, so should the preferences and experiences be. Regardless of the choice or method to obtain, maintain and enhance fitness, proper form, correct posture and good technique is a must to reap the true benefits and sustain from any long term discomfort and/or injury. Get motivated, get educated and get fit.

Sleep

Sleep, as common as it is, for many, it is in short abundance. Sleep is one of the most overlooked and underappreciated human abilities and needs there is. Proper rest offers not only the body, but everything else – mind, emotion and spirit, countless benefits. Sleep deprivation robs the mind of clear and concise thought – making the ability to carry out high cognitive tasks difficult, steals from the body energy and strength, weakens the emotions and extinguishes the spirit. Under stressful situations, sleep deprivation can render a responder ineffective and vulnerable – placing not only the life of the patient at further risk but their own as well.

Lack of sleep lowers our immune system leaving us susceptible to viruses and illness. Sleep is our natural way for regeneration and rejuvenation – on a daily basis. Immune, nervous, skeletal and muscular systems all refresh while we sleep. Sleep is a mood compass – the less we have the more of a bad mood we will be in.

Responders/Rescuers run long hour and sometimes multiple shifts that can easily wear down an individual's energy and reserves. So it is not uncommon to see such professionals running on empty – consistently. We should consider sleep as a loan. We spend that loan throughout the day and when we run out of sleep, we start to build up a sleep debt. The body will want to collect on that debt eventually. If your body requires 6 hours of sleep per night to perform optimally, and you only get four, then each night you build up a 2 hour sleep debt. At some time, the body will collect...in some way, and somehow. It will involuntarily begin to shut down processes in order to minimize energy use as it is starved for needed rest. At some point in time, if unresolved sleep deprivation can become a life-threatening condition as the body has shut down enough processes to disrupt homeostasis. Ample sleep is required for optimal peak performance therefore periodic naps during a shift can be of use if normal sleeping patterns are inconsistent or interrupted. Find time to sleep.

Resilience Training

The human mind is like a rubber band with regards to stress and recovery. It must be wound (addition of negative stress) and released with equal and regular frequency (oscillating pattern) in order for it to remain "resilient" or "elastic" per se. With the unpredictability of the nature of calls most emergency providers encounter, most have developed compensatory mechanisms which allow them to cope with the pre-incident stress, boredom and anticipation that are all part of the job. However, this state of persistent stress interrupts the "oscillating" pattern of stress and recovery. Like a rubber band that has been wound tight and kept that way, the EMS provider's ability to "snap back" (resiliency) is compromised. As resiliency decreases, fatigue increases, and overall performance and physical capacity suffer, therefore attention must be paid to the spiritual, emotional and physical needs of the rescuer to promote wellness.

Conditioning for improved performance involves the aforementioned "oscillating" pattern between stress and recovery. Resiliency or the ability for an individual to "snap back" to a "baseline" or homeostasis is based on interval patterns of stress and recovery. Keeping in mind the requirement for the body to recover (or regenerate positive energy), if the body is under a constant state of stress (cumulative), it does not have the ability to recover or regenerate its positive energy stores, therefore resulting in chronic fatigue, burnout and adverse physical manifestations.

Spirituality is often viewed as controversial in the workplace and as having no real relevance to performance and is more often viewed as a discussion of religion rather than individual motivation. Students of leadership must understand what motivates a group to follow a leader. Leadership is a cultural trait and not a commodity that can be "bottled" and distributed therefore good leaders must undertand cultures of their organizations and what motivates their people. Leaders exist in avery facet of life, from parents in a family to the top generals in the military and CEO's of industry. In most cases of truly inspirational leadership, there is a connection between the leader and followers. That connectivity is based on many factors, but one of those is spiritual. That spiritual connection, or motivation that inspires the soldier to commit heinous acts in combat; or motivates the rescuer to run into a collapsing tower while everyone passes him on their way out. This motivation is seeded in one's deepest personal values, and the discussion of spirtuality is really the examination of what gives the individual their sense of purpose, and is not necessarily focused on any religious factors. In order to foster this continuum of motivation, considerations for the adverse effects of stress on spirituality must be considered and addressed.

Various leaders in industry have sought to increase the performance of personnel within their organizations. The search for the perfect performance state involves improving endurance, positive motivation and intellectual clarity. In the traditional corporate world, personnel are typically challenged more in the intellectual tasks and responsibilities however healthcare, public safety and military personnel have a much wider requirement for all aspects of physical, mental and emotional performance measures. Emergency workers are often equally challenged in their occupations through physical endurance as much as they are intellectual tasks. Due to the nature of emergency response, there seems to be no real mechanisms available to predict which of the performance criteria will be the most challenged and when they will be challenged.

The physical demands of emergency medical services can be intense as it frequently involves bending, lifting, stooping and body movements in unnatural and unpredictable ways. The primarily sedentary nature of the occupation frequently causes extended periods of downtime in which the emergency worker fails to exercise or participate in wellness activities. Physical fitness or wellness programs implemented in corporations have shown success in enhancing both physical as well as intellectual performance in workers. A robust, regular and controlled exercise and wellness program within public safety organizations will likely yield positive results to overall organizational goals.

The long-term positive effects of physical exercise and wellness programs on emotional wellness of soldiers have been demonstrated by the military in resilience training research. In modern military training a focus on total mind-body wellness training includes a regular physical training program accompanied by regular awareness education on occupation-

Rescuer Mindset

specific stress issues faced by service members not only during war, but also in peacetime. Similar approaches to training and wellness should be implemented into public safety in order to reduce the stress-casualty rates.

Spiritual & Emotional Fitness ✟

Maintaining Spiritual and Emotional Weight
From a social American standpoint, much focus in the fitness world is about losing or maintaining a healthy weight. With so many delicious and convenient food distractions, we find ourselves in the midst of a weight issue – there always seem to be temptations. Whether we eat out of boredom, for emotional comfort, or we have some medical issues that keep the pounds on, many people struggle with maintaining optimum weight levels.

The same holds true for our emotional and spiritual health. In many respects, talking about or sharing emotional and spiritual beliefs is quite a private matter, expressed in the presence of a select few so as not to offend or feel vulnerable. At times we forget how intertwined our physical health is with that of our emotional and spiritual health. Our emotional and spiritual weight fluctuates based on our experiences, diet, amount of sleep, mindset, interactions, relationships, self worth and a whole bunch of other factors.

For instance, if you're having a bad day, have you ever stopped yourself in the middle of your day and noticed how

Rescuer Mindset

exhausted you were? Have you ever considering stopping yourself at all – just for a moment – maybe to reflect on why you may be having a bad day? Do you ever take the time to determine why you were tired? The reasoning stumps a lot of people especially if they've just come off a great night's sleep. Stress and tension can be very taxing. There's a lot being processed in our bodies every minute of every day, so sometimes we need to give our bodies a little makeover, some slack, or a bit of attention just to keep everything running properly.

We have all been told one of the best ways to nurture ourselves is to ingest more of the natural supplements available to us. Sure we may need an extra multivitamin here and there during our week, but what would be most efficient is including the natural, easy items like water, fruits and vegetables consistently throughout our day. Eating a snack of fruits or vegetables refreshes us not only physically but mentally and emotionally as well. Rather than being weighed down with the extended process of digesting the chemicals, sugar and additional calories found in a candy bar, bag of chips or handful of cheese crackers, the body quickly extracts the nutrients needed from the fruit or vegetable and sends the rest away as liquid waste. Eating healthily lifts our spirits as well as our emotional aspect and self-image. We know and believe we are healthy because we are making an effort to consume healthy substances. We can also digest other natural supplements to enhance our spiritual and emotional health. Natural supplements like love, kindness, compassion, trust, laughter and positive words and actions do wonders for us all. Kindness and love shown or given in word or action is kindness and love received. Laughter is the universal gesture of happiness and joy. Laughter invokes a sense of acceptance and provides a positive emotional and spiritual release or shift. Laughter allows us to express us. All things need the natural substances of life for quality of life to be experienced.

There will be times, though, when even the best natural substances may not be enough – self interaction is needed. Whether or not we are emotional or spiritually heavy will have the greatest impact on any situation based on how we choose to deal with whatever comes our way. For instance, one winter day, car issues make us late for work, our manager berates us for tardiness, expresses a negative opinion about a work project, and a couple projects we're working on face continual delays regardless of any efforts to keep things on track. After a few hours

Rescuer Mindset

of being in that non-encouraging energy, we may drive home with a negative, heavy mindset. Once we arrive at home, we are met with a heater that has stopped working.

Since we were already in a state of mind, emotion, and spirit that is down in the dumps, where self esteem and self worth were being questioned, when realizing that a big ticket household appliance is broken, we may respond in an angry outburst, or swell into a copious dose of depression – a knee jerk reaction to what we may have considered as another threat to our abilities or character. We have now projected our mood and feelings to our environment and the people in it – becoming a domino effect.

Now, if we had had a great day at work where everything was going really well – the car started great, heard a favorite song on the way in, our projects were within budget and on time, praise was given, etc, and the same heater was not working when we arrived home, we'd likely approach and respond to that situation with much more objectivity than in the previous scenario.

How do we maintain a healthy emotional and spiritual weight, where we ward off the heaviness and stay lighthearted? First, we need to be aware of what our ideal emotional and spiritual weight is. Emotionally, we need to know (or determine if we don't already know) where our emotional level is. We need to know what raises and what decreases our emotional levels. We need to know when we are able to give more and when we aren't capable of giving as much. We need to be able and willing to receive assistance when necessary and be open to ask for it as well. We need to know when we're feeling good and when we're not, and then accurately communicate those feelings to those around us so they can plan for, approach, and blend with us differently if they so choose. We can create acceptable space so everyone benefits rather than forming an unexpected collision.

This all begins with awareness – awareness of how we are feeling in each given moment – taking notice to when we're "off" versus when we are "on". There's a common philosophy to only give of your overflow. So, figuratively speaking, if our emotional cup or bucket is full, then it's easy to participate in emotionally charged events without depleting ourselves too much. However, if our emotional cup or bucket is half full, those same emotionally charged events will affect us completely differently, potentially depleting any reserves we had, causing us to potentially unnecessarily lash out at others.

Rescuer Mindset

To maintain our emotional levels at optimum weight, we need to explore, consider, and act upon activities or non activities that we find replenish our emotional selves. There are many times when this is not as possible due to timing, finances, and other such obstacles that may present themselves. However, there is another way for us to maintain our emotional levels in the moment while practicing awareness. Our thoughts are great monitors of our mindset and feelings. What our thoughts are at a given moment directly affect our emotional and spiritual state. If we have better control at guiding our thoughts towards more positive outlets, we can see and feel major differences in our demeanor, even after only a few seconds or minutes of focus. It does take time and practice, however, it can be done. We just have to want and believe for it to occur.

If we happen to be having a difficult conversation with someone – rather than thinking about how obstinate they are or how we can never seem to agree on anything, change our thoughts to send out good vibes, even if the thoughts are just one or two words. If we think love, harmony, and/or cooperation, our mindset changes, which may work to effectively change the other person's mindset as well without doing anything more or different. As we change they change. We allow that thought of love, harmony and cooperation to be open and free. It now can do its job. And if nothing more, it will help alleviate our initial frustration of working with that person and makes that interaction emotionally and spiritually acceptable.

From a spiritual level – we all do wonderful things to help boost our own spirits – we watch funny movies, spend time with family and friends, tell each other jokes, go for a bike ride, horse ride, or fly an airplane. We take vacations, hike in the woods, garden, bake, play games, get a massage or other energy work, meditate, etc. We all have our own unique or not so unique ways to lift ours spirits up tremendously. Again, we don't always feel we have the time to devote to our spiritual health, but we can take little steps along the way.

For instance, focusing on enhancing and deepening our breath is a wonderful way to clear our thoughts, filter through some emotions, and make way for our spirit to shine through. Taking a walk, a bath or being near a body of water is extremely cleansing as well. Any of these sorts of things can be done in a short spurt of time throughout the day – as long as we know what

Rescuer Mindset

they are and make them a part of what we do when we are able to.

Surrounding ourselves with people who inspire and enjoy life is essential for a healthy spiritual being. Those who may lower our spirits with negative thoughts, actions and words can be detrimental to our growth and sustainability for emotional and spiritual success. It may be that these individuals have not been shown love, compassion or kindness. They cannot demonstrate what they have not experienced. An assessment of their willingness to embrace such natural substances may lead to a change of heart and mind. The domino effect continues on. We touch lives and others touch ours. It is the circle of life – the circle of being.

Our all around well being is essential to the health of our selves – the health of our lives. Taking into all aspects of our human existence – physical, mental, emotional, and spiritual – will only enhance the ways in which we choose to spend our time and who we are while we live.

Mindset for Meditation

Each day we are bombarded with various energies not only surrounding us but also within us. Externally, we are affected by the colors of clothes and lights, the shapes of furniture and wall hangings, the sound waves from music, alarms, transportation vehicles, radios, the electromagnetic waves from phones, power lines, computers, and other electronic devices; and the emotional energy trail of everyone who comes within our physical or mental eyesight – close or far away. Internally we filter through our own emotions, judgments, thoughts, and perceptions that add into an already potentially overloaded system.

We all know what it feels like when we've reached our threshold of being able to adequately handle, from our personal

Rescuer Mindset

perspective, what comes our way. Most of us know when we should ask for help or choose to take a break – whether it is a five minute step away from a situation or a five day retreat or vacation. At these times, we take note in some way of our energy levels – our physical state, mental capacity, and emotional well being. Some of us are very aware of why and how we've reached the breaking point. Some of us just know it's time for a break and accept it is part of a cycle we live in.

What happens to us is that we allow all the energies we're bombarded with daily to pile up and weigh down our energetic structure – our physical, emotional, mental, and spiritual bodies. (Let this author take a moment to explain the spiritual body. To this author, every living human has a spirit. This spirit is likened to a soul or abstract structure of light or energy that exists within and around the human body. In this author's perspective, the spirit is simply that boundary beyond the physical body that houses the connection or ability to connect with all that is "heartful." The spirit is not associated with a religion – it is something we are born with. The spirit is not to be confused with one's personality, although the spirit can influence one's personality traits.)

As days and weeks pass, simply by existing, we expose our energetic bodies to all sorts of energetic traffic. Sometimes that traffic builds up to a point where our energy flow becomes blocked or jammed. Our energetic bodies are really quite intelligent, so if there is an energetic traffic jam somewhere, our energy immediately attempts to find another flow route. This alternative flow route may be simple to create or it can be quite complex, depending upon our state of being at that moment. Sometimes, the energy doesn't find an alternative flow route and stagnates. This stagnation can manifest itself as some type of pain or discomfort in any of our energetic bodies. Many of us successfully suppress or ignore the mental or emotional cues that something is out of alignment and tend to wait until the physical body is affected before we consider taking some down time and focusing on us for a while.

As human beings, we are very talented at putting things in the proverbial drawers within our mind – into an emotional cabinet structure. We file things away for reference later. The issue arises if we filed these items without carefully reviewing them to determine if they're even worth keeping. Sometimes we may reference these items later, but we need to be careful if those

Rescuer Mindset

references help us or hinder us. Past experiences that harbor dissidence and hatred for someone or something still maintain the emotional heaviness of the experience itself. The question becomes: are we able to learn from this experience, and take only a mental statement from that experience and then shred the file?

Much of our mental and emotional file cabinets are filled with items that we simply haven't taken or made the time to process thoroughly. These items were filed after a quick second or two judgment with minor internal discussion. The more we choose to store in our energetic filing cabinets, the more easily the energetic bodies tend to get clogged; the more easily we grow impatient with others or the more quickly we get tired on any level. Many of us tend to masquerade as soldiers for ourselves, protecting our experiences, – especially our hurts – as reasons to possess and nurture certain negative characteristics, or as an excuse not to move forward with something. By addressing our true feelings about experiences or a situation, the less filing we need to do in our energetic filing cabinets.

Unfortunately, Americans live in a society that openly purports that being in touch with one's feelings is considered weak, and even effeminate. Being effeminate is simply not acceptable. Interestingly, a common misnomer is that being in touch with our feelings means we need to be all mushy and loveable. This is not so. More often than not, what it comes down to is facing some personal fears we have about ourselves or about the world we live in. We all know that the best way to overcome our fears is to confront them head on – baby steps or mountain trekking to face them. The sooner we do, the sooner we get past them.

Getting in touch with our feelings simply means we know and can identify the emotion or emotions we are experiencing. It also means we can begin to explore why we feel that way. And why we feel a certain way usually surpasses the external factors of a situation and delves a little deeper in search of the internal flags and insecurities that were raised by the situation. One sure fire way to identify our feelings is to truly ponder them. Many of us won't need to ponder long – we know what we're feeling. Some of us, though, will need to allow ourselves time to accurately identify the base feeling. Some of us have been so ingrained to suppress any emotion at all, that allowing the emotion to flow to the surface where we can actually identify it, may be a bit difficult.

Rescuer Mindset

By pondering our emotions and reasons for the emotions, we are actually on our first step to meditating on them. Sometimes we can't identify why we're feeling a certain way – and sometimes we may not need to know why. Learning how we operate internally on a thought process and emotional level really is beneficial when walking through high stress situations or after experiencing them.

Meditation is something we've all done before – meditation can be a deep reflection on a specific issue or problem – where the focus is on one point with the intent to find a solution, answer a question, or work through emotions. It doesn't matter what the end result is per say, rather it is more the method of clearing the mind to have one focus or no focus. The true issue with meditation is taking adequate time to reflect on things that need reflection. Our jobs and lives can be quite hectic and scattered that making the time to ponder, reflect, and meditate is not always a high priority. There are many folks out there with "normal" lives and "normal" stresses – but when bombarded with stressful occurrences in a short timeframe, people tend to reach a breaking point. As our energetic traffic jams up, it is incredibly helpful to be aware that a block up is happening. The human energy field accepts and filters energy waves 24 x 7. There is no break in this process unless we make one.

The easiest way to take a break anywhere, at any time, is to simply close our eyes wherever we are, and take a deep breath... or four or five. See how the body and mind respond to this simple breathing exercise. Then, the next step would be to take three to five minutes and only focus on the breath. The breaths need not be deep breaths, the intent is simply to focus on the breath. It may be surprising at how many thoughts cross the mind, and that's ok, it's a matter of bringing the mind then back to focusing on our breathing pattern. By giving the mind something to focus on – the breath – we train the mind to limit or cease thinking. As a result of this process, our physical body rests and our emotional body flows with less mental restrictions and an overall sense of peace begins to move through the energetic bodies.

Meditation lifts the weight and heaviness of our energetic body build up. Meditation helps clear the physical, emotional, and mental traffic jams. Through the simple focus on our breath which many meditation practices start with, our physical body relaxes, our emotional body expands, our minds start to clear,

Rescuer Mindset

and our spirit becomes open to a broader perspective. This breathing then heightens our process flow when reflecting on our day's events. The reflection/meditation helps bring to the surface some of the thoughts and emotions we suppressed in order to continue to get through our day. By completely immersing ourselves in the mind–body–spirit connection, we release energetic blocks and allow our energy to flow, providing further clarity and rejuvenation.

Through meditation we will find that we are less aware of our bodies than we believe ourselves to currently be. Some of us claim we are unable to sit still for 15 minutes of time to mediate traditionally. Meditation can be learned. It is something we must give ourselves time to adapt to. Sitting in the stillness (regardless of timeframe) gives us the opportunity to truly be with ourselves with no distractions. Starting off with simple and with short timeframes increases the likelihood of successfully incorporating meditation into our lives. Once we do start meditating regularly, we start to realize how clear, energized, and "ready" we are for our daily tasks and we notice the times when we skip meditating.

Responders are exposed to intense situations, emotions, harsh words, and high stress environments. While there are dangers and stresses in every job, as well as the factor of the human condition, our bodies react subconsciously to the on goings around us. Remaining stable during these on goings is truly a service to ourselves and one another. Meditation has been proven to enhance the physical recovery of injuries, assist in curing disease or living with illnesses, help with pain management and increase the success of surgical procedures. Meditation has helped decrease depression and anxiety, and assists people through emotional trauma or emotional difficulties. Meditation can clear the mind to be open to solutions or creativity not previously experienced. On a spiritual level, if desired, meditation can help one experience nirvana, God, or oneness.

If we consider our bodies as energy vessels that can carry and hold wanted as well as unwanted energy, we can look to meditation as the filter or cleanser of the energetic masses in, through, and around us. Meditation allows us the option for a regular full spring cleaning or a periodic window washing. Whichever level we choose, our bodies on all levels notice a difference not only in the way we hold ourselves and interact with others, but also how it affects the way in which we perceive our world. Meditation becomes our mediator, our tool, for which we

Rescuer Mindset

communicate with ourselves – growing and learning all the while, inside and out.

Stress Management

Managing Stressors

Stress is described as the inability to respond appropriately to emotional, mental and even physical overload so often found in today's world. Stress has many forms and the management of its effects varies as well. Each of us confronts and deals with stress differently. Stress management is a learned response. Initially, we learned how to cope by watching others. Often, family members will deal with stress inoculation in similar fashions. However, since it is a learned response, we can learn effective means to properly handle these periodic overloads.

There are many types of stress – physical stress, emotional stress, and mental stress. Each type of stress not only affects the specific area of impact, but also aggravates or depletes the other aspects as well. For instance, if a corporate worker puts in three 12-hour days of focused, intense meetings and documentation, you can bet that by the end of that third day their mental capacity is rather fried. After an overload of meetings and grueling focus, upon arriving home or at a restaurant for dinner afterwards, the conversation at the end of day three will be either quite minimal or limited in thought process. The mental

Rescuer Mindset

body had been stressed for an extended period of time, and it is in need of a rest. As a result the physical body will be quite tired as well, even though all the body did physically during those three days was digest food and sit in a chair or stand in front of a group of people for a presentation.

The emotional aspects and attachments to the perceived success of the meetings and presentation also played a role in taxing the mental and physical aspects of the body. So by the end of day three, we have one exhausted individual who really doesn't want to do much of anything but possibly get some sleep and potentially a beverage of choice. One large stressor can affect all human aspects – our mental clarity, emotional and spiritual fitness, and physical energy levels.

Stress exists in two forms – positive and negative. Positive stress is the type that is exhilarating and healthy. These short-term episodes boost creative thinking and thought and allow the mind and body a release helping to improve dispositions. Exercise and problem solving tasks at home or work are examples of positive stress. Negative stress is the type that overtaxes our mind and body to a degree that it becomes unhealthy – causing our systems to fall out of balance and begin to malfunction.

Experiencing long periods of chronic stress forces our systems to go into protect mode and possibly even shutting down. Some common effects of short or long term stress include headaches, raised heart rate, exhaustion, difficulty concentrating, muscle soreness and tension, mood swings, over eating, memory issues, decreased sex drive, sleep disorders, and addictions.

One of the first things doctors or other folks may tell us to alleviate stress is to decrease the number of stress factors in our lives. This is a great initial approach – to see where we may be over extending ourselves perhaps unnecessarily. We have the opportunity then to consider making some minor adjustments, perhaps rely on other people a bit more, or let go of some responsibility that is not pertinent to our life survival. Accept the things we cannot change.

This initial life stressor evaluation can be extremely helpful to everyone. Although we may strive for stress free lives, so long as we have attachments to goals, conversations, relationships, material aspects, life itself, etc., some levels of stress are typically something that we can accept as part of our lives. Without some of the positive stressors in our lives we would

Rescuer Mindset

feel no challenge, limited growth, potentially be bored, and even more potentially make up things to do or stress about.

Perspective and awareness can change how we view and how we react to stress. First, it's important to note what stress feels like. For instance, positive stress may be excitement, challenging, looking forward to something with great anticipation, learning and focusing on a specific topic or skill.   Negative stress feels as though our muscles are tense, our breath is shallow, overwhelming, or perhaps a pit or knot in the stomach. Once we realize how the stress feels to us, we can combat it with exercises or paths of least resistance to get through it. Some of us also know specific situations or interactions that provide stress time and again. While we can take the road of avoiding the situation or interaction as much as possible, avoidance may not always be possible.

Common ways to relieve stress include taking vacations, meditating, walking, exercising, or getting a massage. Other potential methods for dealing with our stressors are to talk about them with trusted friends and family or journal about them. Journaling can be very therapeutic. Listening to good music is helpful as is spending time with pets or small children. Their carefree in the moment attitudes help to see the world in an innocent yet wondrous light. Acceptance of situations that we have no control over is extremely freeing as well.

Rescuer Mindset

Intuition

Feel Your Way Around

As we come full circle with our daily lives; the people we meet, the jobs we do, the tasks we accomplish, the answers we seek, the difference we make, we come to realize that so much more is involved and so much more exists. By our very own existence we acknowledge the existence of not only others but other possibilities, other realities and other visions of what life can hold for us. What we see is not what's always on the surface – it is not always what we get.

What is not on the surface cannot always be seen by our eyes. It is a matter of feeling – of intuition. More is out there and it does exist. Though many of us are taught that seeing is believing the truth is really in the belief that believing is seeing." Belief is a feeling that there is more. Simply believe and we will see, not just with our eyes, but with our heart and mind, to what is really before us. Believing has the power to move mountains and divide seas. Believing is feeling all that is, all that exists, all that we are and all that we will be. Believing is feeling and feeling *is* believing.

Rescuer Mindset

Intuition is a fervent and swift insightful interpretation of a given situation or circumstance. As a definition used in theoretical contexts, intuition is a sort of belief being rooted in personal experience. Intuition comes from the Latin meaning to *look inside.* Of course someone can have an intuitive view when all the facts of the outcome are looming before them and it is a matter of connecting the dots. But the kind of intuition we are discussing is the gut feeling or hunch instinct. Everyone possesses this sixth sense ability whether admitting to it or not. It is the unspoken, innate human ability many of us tend to disregard or refuse to enable when things seem amiss.

The notion of feeling should not be confused with feelings as related to emotions. Though at times, intuition can create sensations and enhance emotions during such experiences as that it speaks through these channels, alerting us of the real intent of things or people. This sub-conscious, internal process takes place in not only the right side of the brain but also in the heart – heart, referring not to the organ itself but rather the internal spirit – the soul, the being – of and in each of us. As rescuers/Responders, before one can truly heal, one must be able to feel.

Intuition is lightning fast. Its reflex to assess a situation in the blink of an eye stacks itself heads and shoulders above the five main senses, which at times can become distracted and clouded causing a misinterpretation or oversight. With any encounter there exists a dynamic of energy.

This energy fills the air and resonates with everyone and everything that surrounds you. That energy is the glue, so to speak, that holds things together or the oil that keeps everything running smoothly. It is a balanced entity. When that energy balance is shifted or polluted with negative intentions a misalignment in the field occurs. That misalignment can be felt.

The ongoing theme throughout this book has been awareness. Being aware puts you in the mix – it makes you a major player. Awareness affords you the chance to have the deck stacked in your favor regardless of the other players. Intuition is just another part, another level, of awareness. All levels of awareness can be honed and enhanced, as described in the *Sensory Perception Training* (S.P.T.) and *Awareness Training* sections in previous chapters. Theoretically, intuition is enhanced simply by experience but the notion that experience alone will carry you may not be such a safe bet.

Rescuer Mindset

What are your experiences and how do they lend to an increase of awareness? As the experiences you have increase your intuitive abilities to a degree, it is the types/kinds of experiences you have that will define the sensitivity of your intuition. Though everyone will not experience the same forms of experiences even in the same experience, higher levels of intuitive cognizance can be achieved. Reach out and feel. Not just by touch but by looking beyond. It is those subtle things, those quiet things, and those unspoken things, the things you feel that make the difference and tell the whole truths. Each experience has truths, as they are a part of everything we encounter. We just need to look for them and be open to what they have to tell us – we need to be aware. Intuition is insight into infinity.

With every call, with every emergency, with every encounter, awareness, and deeper, our intuition, is at work. Our personal process by which we obtain information to find a solution: awareness, intuition and experience compounded together. The presence of information can be as simple as a phrase spoken, a gesture made, an action taken or even simpler the lack thereof. Intuition then becomes an accumulation of knowledge – knowledge gained by awareness and experience. It is a built-in informational highway that our forefathers called *self-evident truth*. We start at a base and over time we expound our minds, our senses and our feelings to increase and intensify our experience, which opens our awareness, which develops our intuition. If, though, at the moment experience is in short supply, intuition can become its own guide. The power of your intuition is in direct relation to your connection to the moment – the here and now.

Parents, especially mothers, are uniquely connected to their children. From the time of conception, during the term in the womb, to the day of birth and beyond, most mothers are forever linked in, connected to, their children. Many of us have stories of a parent who was able to know when something was amiss or when the child was about to do something that would have been classified as "stupid" or that could harm us in some way. It is a double connection – it is a connection of the heart – where love is free, open and unconditional and it is a connection of mind – where brain waves and frequencies are in tune and aligned.

This connection is also present in siblings and has been documented in cases involving twins. The connection is known to

Rescuer Mindset

exist in couples who have been together for a number of years or among individuals who have share a great episode in life such as soldiers and survivor victims.

This connection does not have to be strictly gene or shared tragedy related either. Individuals who have lead a less than luxurious life filled with their share of trials and tribulations often display an insight into a world not many experience. This insight allows them to "get it", upping their connection two-fold as they are able to relate on a variety of levels to a variety of situations and human conditions, thus, working on a different wave length than the average person. Their experience along with their now heightened sense of intuition coupled with their extreme awareness capabilities creates a vacuum of information and perception to define and refine solutions for just about anything.

Intuition is all but useless if not acted upon when it is either called on or when it takes the initiative to become our beacon. The ability to trust what we feel creates a clear path for our intuition to excel. Trusting our feelings is trusting our integrity to know what is right and when things are off. It is trusting in ourselves unconditionally – which is just another form of love – self love. The inner guidance of our intuition is not about "what you can't do," but rather "what you can do," and about whom you can become. Intuition is a universal linking to something greater than the individual themselves. Rules and standards do not apply. If it feels right, without a doubt, without the slightest inkling of wonder, hesitation or question, then it must be right – it is the inner you lighting the way for the outer you. When you and another experience true love it is that trust that set the tone and leads the way – like being on auto-pilot – you just know. As previously mentioned trust is the ability to listen, and listening is a deeper awareness. Listen to what you have to say to yourself – you may be surprised of how much you can learn.

Intuition can be improved upon – it can he enhanced. For your own sense of experiment and adventure to develop your intuition simply try something different. Something you have not done before. Allow what you feel to be your guide as you take in the newness and freshness of this first time experience. This is, of course, a controlled experiment where at anytime things become unnerving or potentially catastrophic; you can just pull the plug. Or, you can allow your intuition to prompt questions for answers that may fill in the blanks. Our intuition will grow as we grow –

Rescuer Mindset

learning along the way. However, its ability to process without apprehension (fear) and with apprehension (understanding) will out shine our outward abilities.

What this demonstrates is a chance for you to *go with the flow* and let what happens now, lead you into the next – the future. This allows you to follow what you believe and what you trust. Let intuition be your guide. Intuition can be a great asset. Intuition is another way to assess and apply what a Rescuer/Responder does. It is yet another level and facet of awareness. It is another level and facet of trust. It is another level and facet of you.

Conclusion

Discovering the multitude of possibilities that exist for any one encounter can be staggering. Realizing that we are capable of interpreting these possibilities on many levels is also just as staggering. As professionals, it becomes your duty to not only become aware of the possibilities but refrain from allowing the confrontation of each possibility not to sway you from performing your service and task. You have been called upon both by community and creation to uphold what countless individuals before you have made their life's mission – duty, service and justice. These three virtues are what make anyone, who rushes to the needs of another, a pillar of the community, leaving their mark on society so the world is made safer and better with each passing day of their existence. Duty is the life we choose. Service is the life we make. And justice is the life we seek. The duty is to ourselves, where the service is to others, while yet still the justice is for all. When one begins the journey of such magnitude, each virtue seems to be a separate entity. As time unfolds and the journey takes us further down the path, we come to learn that these three virtues are inter-connected, and, they are actually

Rescuer Mindset

one in the same. It is not common that the paths we seek and choose to follow, the ones less traveled, are often the ones that demand the most self sacrifice – family, friends, time, energy. And yet with all that self sacrifice comes an even greater reward, the reward of making a difference. Though it may go unnoticed and even less demonstrated with appreciation, in your heart of hearts, where it really counts, you know you have made the difference of a lifetime.

Rescuers/Responders are a unique breed, but no different a breed than as those who give of themselves so that others may live a fulfilling life. The daily demands placed upon each emergency professional, as the war of illness, age and accident wages on the peoples of the world, are great, they are many and they can be taxing. But the soldiers of this war band together, finding absolution and resolution in the work they do and with each other. It is a brotherhood and it is a family. It is a legacy and it is a heritage. The lineage has been passed down through time and yet it is timeless. The message is timeless – serving others serves you. Selfless or selfish? For Rescuers/Responders there is a difference. The difference is you and the difference saves many.

Bibliography

Aloia, M. (2009). *How Aikido Can Change the World*, Aloia Publishing.

Aloia, M. (2010). *Essential Basics of Self Defense*, Aloia Publishing.

Aloia, M. (2011). *Converging of Energies – Aikido's Path of Least Resistance*, March Baby Publishing.

Aloia, P. (2009 First edition – 2011 Second Edition). *52 Pick Me Up*, March Baby Publishing.

American Heart Association. (2010, January 01). *Stress and Heart Disease*. Retrieved October 19, 2010, from American Heart Association: http://www.americanheart.org/presenter.jhtml?identifier=4750

Avena, N., Rada, P., & Hoebel, B. (2008). Evidence for sugar addiction: behavioral and neurochemical effects of intermittent, excessive sugar intake. *Journal of Neuroscience and Biobehavior*, 20-39.

Barling, J., Kelloway, K. E., & Frone, M. R. (2005). *Handbook of Work Stress*. Thousand Oaks: Sage Publications, Inc.

Rescuer Mindset

Bennett, P., Williams, Y., Page, N., Hood, K., Woollard, M., & Vetter, N. (2005). Associations Between Organizational and Incident Factors and Emotional Distress in Emergency Ambulance Personnel. *The British Journal of Clinical Psychology*, 215-226.

Bjorn-Ove, S. (2002). Ambulance Responses at a Disaster Site. *Emergency Nurse*, 22-27.

Cooper, C. L., & Dewe, P. (2004). *Stress: A Brief History.* Padstow: Blackwell Publishing.

Grossman, D., & Christensen, L. (2004). *On Combat: The Psychology and Physiology of DeadlyConflict in War and In Peace.* Portland: PPCT Research Publications.

Hufford, D. J., Fritts, M. J., & Rhodes, J. E. (2010). Spiritual Fitness. *Military Medicine*, 73-87.

Journal of Emergency Medical Services. (2010, October 01). *2010 EMS Salary & Workplace Survey.* Retrieved October 19, 2010, from Journal of Emergency Medical Services: http://www.jems.com/article/salary-survey/2010-jems-salary-workplace-sur

Kyle, S. N. (2007). First Responders Recall Virginia Tech Tragedy. *EMS Responder*, 16-17.

Loehr, J., & Schwartz, T. (2001). The Making of a Corporate Athlete. *Harvard Business Review,* 120-128.

Lowery, K., & Stokes, M. A. (2005). Role of Peer Support and Emotional Expression on Posttraumatic Stress Disorder in Student Paramedics. *Journal of Traumatic Stress*, 171- 179.

Ludwig, G. (2006). Three Phases of Being a Paramedic. *Firehouse*, 44-45.

Mullen, M. (2010). On Total Force Fitness in War and Peace. *Military Medicine*, 1-2.

Newsome, B. (2003). The Myth of Intrinsic Combat Motivation. *The Journal of Strategic Studies*, 24-26.

Powers, R. (2007). Employee Retention: Applying Hospital Strategies to EMS. *EMS Responder*, 100-104.

Regehr, C. (2005). Bringing the Trauma Home: Spouses of Paramedics. *Journal of Loss and Trauma*, 97-114.

Regehr, C., Goldberg, G., Glancy, G. D., & Knott, T. (2002). Posttraumatic Symptoms and Disability in Paramedics. *Canadian Journal of Psychiatry*, 953-958.

Rubin, M. (2009). Dealing with Downtime. *EMS Responder*, 65-70.

Rubin, M. (2010). Sharing the Burden. *EMS Responder*, 74.

Rescuer Mindset

Scott, T. (2007). Expression of Humour by Emergency Personnel Involved in Sudden Death Work. *Mortality*, 350-364.

Swinhart, D. (2007). Can't Get No Satisfaction. *EMS Responder*, 172-174.

US Army Surgeon General. (2003). *Mental Health Advisory Team (MHAT)*. Bethesda: US Army.

About the Authors

Michael Aloia is martial arts instructor and personal trainer with schools in Pennsylvania. He conducts workshops and clinics on personal safety and defense as well as group leadership classes. His research has brought him to produce the *Aikido – art in motion* DVD series and the *Essential Defense* DVD series which includes the book *Essential Basics of Self Defense*. Michael is also the author of the books *How Aikido Can Change the World* and *Converging of Energies – Aikido's Path of Least Resistance*. He writes articles and publishes several monthly newsletters. Michael enjoys playing guitar and working as an artist.

Brian P. Pasquale, MPH, NREMT-P is a PhD student specializing in emergency management at Capella University. He earned his Master's degree in Public Health from American Military University while still serving in the military. He retired after 22 years of Army Reserve service, spending his last 12 years in Army Special Operations. Brian has been a paramedic since 1990. He has been teaching emergency medical services rescuer programs since the 1990's and has taught hundreds of deploying soldiers since the beginning of GWOT operations in 2001. He served as a flight medic during Operation Desert Storm and served stateside in support of current GWOT Operations. Prior to his retirement, Brian was selected to be commissioned as an Army Medical Officer and was awarded the Army Meritorious Service Medal. Brian currently serves as the Executive Director for a local fire company-based EMS unit in Trappe, PA. Brian is currently studying the art of Aikido under the guidance of Aloia Sensei.

Rescuer Mindset

Pamela Aloia holds various certifications in energy modalities including Reiki, Integrated Energy Therapy, Magnified Healing, and Reflexology as well as being a martial arts practitioner. Pamela conducts individual and group sessions and classes on energy awareness, meditation and leadership through her energy center, Sol Angel, in southeastern Pennsylvania and surrounding areas. She understands the need for support and growth in everyone regardless of their path in life. Pamela is the author of the book *52 Pick Me Up* and publishes a regular newsletter for her Sol Angel website and audience.

Authors can be contacted through the following websites:
Michael Aloia: *www.asahidojo.com*
Brian P. Pasquale: *www.rescuermindset.org*
Pamela Aloia: *www.solangel.com*

www.ingramcontent.com/pod-product-compliance
Lightning Source LLC
LaVergne TN
LVHW011417080426
835512LV00005B/115